The AFRICAN ~ AMERICAN Experience

An HBJ Resource Guide for the Multicultural Classroom

HARCOURT BRACE JOVANOVICH, INC.

Orlando Austin San Diego Chicago Dallas New York

LE
185
.1+37
1993

Requests for permission to make copies of any part of the work should be mailed to: Permissions Department, Harcourt Brace Jovanovich, Publishers, 8th Floor, Orlando, Florida 32887

PHOTOGRAPHS: Page 1, Hazel Hankin/Stock, Boston; 51, HBJ/Earl Kogler; 65, HBJ/Maria Paraskevas.

Printed in the United States of America

ISBN 0-15-302010-5

3 4 5 6 7 8 9 10   084   96 95 94 93

Reviewers and Contributors

Nancy L. Arnez is graduate professor of Educational Administration at Howard University and the school's former associate dean, acting dean, and chair of the Department of Educational Leadership. She has written more than 160 educational and creative publications, including the book *The Besieged School Superintendent: A Case Study of School Superintendent–School Board Relations in Washington, D.C., 1973–1975.*

John H. Bracey, Jr., has been a member of the W.E.B. Du Bois Department of Afro-American Studies at the University of Massachusetts, Amherst, for the past two decades, specializing in the history of the African-American experience. In addition to publishing numerous books and articles, Dr. Bracey is coeditor of the Blacks in the New World book series and coeditor of the Black Studies Research Resources microfilm series.

Pat A. Browne is director of African American History/Multicultural Education for the Indianapolis Public Schools. She coordinates the development and implementation of the school district's African-American history curriculum, including staff training. Dr. Browne also is coordinating plans for the Crispus Attucks Museum in Indianapolis, which will feature educational exhibits on the African and African-American experiences.

John Henrik Clarke taught African and world history for more than 20 years and is presently professor emeritus at Hunter College, New York City. He has written or edited more than 27 books on African and African-American history, including *Africans at the Crossroads: Notes for an African World Revolution, Marcus Garvey and His Vision of Africa, New Dimensions in African World History,* and *Malcolm X: The Man and His Times.*

Veleria B. Henson is the principal of John Wesley Dobbs Elementary School in Atlanta, Georgia. Her previous positions with the Atlanta Public Schools include curriculum developer and instructional resource teacher for social studies. She received an Educational Specialist degree from Georgia State University and a Master of Arts from Atlanta University.

Asa G. Hilliard is Fuller E. Callaway Professor of Urban Education at Georgia State University. He is a teacher and educational psychologist with a special interest in African history. Dr. Hilliard is best known as a speaker and leader in the field of multicultural education. He serves as a consultant for the School Department of Harcourt Brace Jovanovich, Inc.

Dianne Johnson teaches children's literature and African-American literature in her home state at the University of South Carolina. She received her Master of Arts in Afro-American Studies and her doctorate in American Studies at Yale University. Dr. Johnson is the author of *Telling Tales: The Pedagogy and Promise of African-American Literature for Youth.*

Faustine C. Jones-Wilson began her career teaching high school history and civics and serving as a school librarian in Gary, Indiana. She is currently acting dean of the School of Education at Howard University. Dr. Jones-Wilson is the author of many articles as well as two books: *The Changing Mood in America: Eroding Commitment?* and *A Traditional Model of Educational Excellence: Dunbar High School of Little Rock, Arkansas.*

Norman McRae is the former director of Fine Arts and Social Studies for the Detroit Public Schools. He has written several books and many articles on the African-American experience and has lectured in history at Wayne State University and the University of Michigan. For the past 18 years Dr. McRae has been a member of the Detroit Historical Commission.

June O. Patton is a professor of History and Public Policy at Governors State University and teaches African-American history at The University of Chicago Laboratory High School. She has taught at the University of Illinois and Roosevelt University in Chicago as well as in several Upward Bound programs. Dr. Patton's most recent published research appears in *The Closing Door: Conservative Policy and Black Opportunity* by Gary Orfield and Carole Ashkinaze.

M. Jackie Perkins is a graduate of Florida A & M University and a retired elementary school teacher. She is the founder and owner of Montsho Books, etc., a bookstore in Orlando, Florida, that specializes in African-American literature and history. (*Montsho* means "black" in Tswana, a dialect spoken in Botswana.) Montsho Books, etc. carries more than 550 titles in children's literature as well as numerous titles for adults.

Christine E. Sleeter is associate professor of Teacher Education at the University of Wisconsin-Parkside. She was formerly a teacher in Seattle, Washington. Dr. Sleeter's main area of interest is multicultural education. She has published numerous articles in various journals as well as several books, including *Empowerment through Multicultural Education* and *Keepers of the American Dream.* She also coauthored *Turning on Learning* and *Making Choices for Multicultural Education* with Carl A. Grant.

Dorothy S. Strickland, the State of New Jersey Professor of Reading, is a former classroom teacher and the author or editor of numerous publications, including *The Administration and Supervision of Reading Programs, Emergent Literacy, Educating Black Children: America's Challenge,* and *Process Reading and Writing.* Dr. Strickland is past president of the International Reading Association.

Sterling Stuckey, professor of History and Religious Studies at the University of California, Riverside, is the author of two books: *Slave Culture* and *The Arts and History.* Dr. Stuckey is currently working on a study of slave labor.

CONTENTS

HOW TO USE THIS GUIDE vi

TO PARENTS AND TEACHERS vii

BOOKS FOR PARENTS AND TEACHERS 1
   Africa and the Caribbean 2
   United States History 7
     Survey Texts, Reference Works, and
      General Overviews 7
     Slavery and Abolition 15
     Free Blacks 21
     The Civil War and Reconstruction 22
     Life at the Turn of the Century 25
     The Twentieth Century 27
     The Civil Rights Movement 30
   Biographies and Autobiographies 34
   The Arts, Sports, and Entertainment 40
   Contemporary Issues 45

RESOURCES FOR MULTICULTURAL EDUCATION 51
   Theory 52
   Practice 57
   Additional References 62

AWARD-WINNING AND NOTABLE BOOKS FOR CHILDREN 65
   Growing Up 66
   The Past 84
   Biographies and Autobiographies 91
   The Arts, Sports, and Entertainment 101
   Seasons and Celebrations 105
   Other Places 107
   Folktales and Legends 112

INDEX OF AUTHORS AND ILLUSTRATORS 120

INDEX OF TITLES 126

The African-American Experience: An HBJ Resource Guide for the Multicultural Classroom is an annotated bibliography of materials that can be useful to parents and teachers interested in multicultural education and in African-American history and culture. The purpose of the guide is to provide an easy-to-use reference that describes books to consult for background information, to help plan lessons, to develop classroom learning centers, or to select for children to read. The guide is not meant to serve as an all-inclusive list of sources. Rather, it offers a sampling of the wealth of material available today.

The guide is divided into three major sections: Books for Parents and Teachers, Resources for Multicultural Education, and Award-Winning and Notable Books for Children. The Books for Parents and Teachers section is divided into several parts, such as Africa and the Caribbean, United States History, and Contemporary Issues. Each part focuses on a different aspect of the African-American experience.

The Resources for Multicultural Education section lists books related to this expanding field. The books in this section are divided into two parts: Theory and Practice. The titles listed under Theory deal primarily with background information and philosophy. The titles listed under Practice offer practical classroom applications, such as lesson plans and teaching ideas.

The Award-Winning and Notable Books for Children section includes works of fiction and nonfiction that are appropriate for children. It is divided into several sections, such as Growing Up, The Past, and Biographies and Autobiographies. Many of the books cited are award winners honored by the Newbery Medal, the Caldecott Medal, or the Coretta Scott King Award. Many also are listed as notable by organizations such as the National Council for the Social Studies. Each entry in the children's section includes the number of pages in the book and the age levels for which it is most appropriate. You may wish to preview the books before recommending them to your students.

The copyright date and publisher given for each book in the guide are for the most recent edition available, whether hardcover or paperback. When appropriate, both the publisher and the imprint are listed, such as Harcourt Brace Jovanovich, Gulliver Books. In a few cases two publishers are listed—the house that currently markets the book and the original publisher. It is hoped that this will facilitate ordering.

A few of the books with older copyrights may be out of print. The authors believe that it is important to remain familiar with some of the classic works in the field that provide valuable insights into current developments. If you find that a book is out of print, check availability with your local library or at a local bookstore.

Classrooms throughout the United States increasingly reflect the cultural diversity of the world. In general, the curriculum does not. The reality is that people all over the world have played a role in the development of human history and culture. It is not necessary to explore the reasons for the low level of awareness of this fact. Rather, it is important to offer support to the thousands of teachers who would attempt to provide a more comprehensive view of human achievement to their students.

Many teachers have already begun to develop supplementary materials to use in their classrooms. Some professional organizations have also taken up this high-priority task. It is important in such a climate and environment that educators be assisted with this vital work.

The African-American Experience: An HBJ Resource Guide for the Multicultural Classroom contains a well-balanced list of resources with annotations that should make the work of educators much easier. Including as it does a general reference list on the African-American experience as well as a list of books suitable for children, this resource guide enables educators to move quickly beyond the rhetoric of multiculturalism to an academically grounded reality base. Any sampling of materials such as this is bound to have its limitations. However, this resource guide succeeds in presenting an excellent range and depth for the content area. It remains for the staff developer to assist educators in becoming familiar with the materials cited and to develop strategies for the infusion of these materials into the regular work that they do.

The work of the teacher is never done. Efforts such as this one suggest the need to provide additional assistance to help educators obtain resources that reflect the broad cultural diversity that is the rich heritage of society. Perhaps this effort will stimulate educators and others to dig deeper and to involve the students themselves in the search for materials that will enhance the curriculum and contribute to an understanding of and respect for all cultural groups.

Asa G. Hilliard, III
Fuller E. Callaway Professor of Urban Education
Georgia State University

Books for Parents and Teachers

Africa and the Caribbean

Ajayi, J.F. Ade, and Michael Crowder, eds. *History of West Africa.* New York: Columbia University Press, 1972.

This collection of articles provides an overview of scholarly assessments of West African history. The work gives special attention to the interaction of economic and political factors during the formation of states. Geographic and demographic maps are included.

Bernal, Martin. *Black Athena.* 2 vols. New Brunswick, N.J.: Rutgers University Press, 1987–1991.

The author presents linguistic and other evidence to document the cultural influences of the Egyptians and Phoenicians on the development of classical Greek civilization. Bernal argues that these influences were purposely overlooked due to European racism and anti-Semitism. Two volumes of a projected three-volume series are currently available.

Bohannan, Paul, and Philip D. Curtin. *Africa and Africans.* 3rd ed. Prospect Heights, Ill.: Waveland Press, 1988.

This straightforward introduction to African cultures offers readers a modern perspective on Africa and its peoples. By providing a synthesis of African traditions as well as of major historical developments, the authors refute common misconceptions about life on the continent.

Curtin, Philip D., ed. *Africa Remembered: Narratives by West Africans from the Era of the Slave Trade.* Madison: University of Wisconsin Press, 1968.

Ten personal narratives examine the slave trade from an African point of view. The thoughts and feelings expressed by those enslaved reflect the richness of the civilizations from which they were forcibly removed.

Davidson, Basil. *The African Genius: An Introduction to Social and Cultural History.* Boston: Little, Brown, 1970.

Like Davidson's other works about Africa, this book is both scholarly and highly readable. *The African Genius* provides a useful analysis of the social and cultural history of the continent.

———. *The African Slave Trade.* Rev. ed. Boston: Little, Brown, 1988.

This study focuses on the enslavement of people in Africa and includes descriptions of both the trans-Atlantic and the trans-Saharan slave trades.

———. *African Civilization Revisited: From Antiquity to Modern Times.* Rev. ed. Trenton: Africa World Press, 1991.

An expanded edition of Davidson's *The African Past: From Antiquity to Modern Times,* this work examines source materials from western, eastern, and southern Africa, emphasizing developments up to the nineteenth century.

De Graft-Johnson, J.C. *African Glory.* Baltimore: Black Classic Press, 1986.

Originally published in 1954, this general history of Africa deals with ancient civilizations and major developments on the entire continent, exploring interrelationships between different regions.

Diop, Cheikh Anta. *The African Origin of Civilization: Myth or Reality?* Edited and translated by Mercer Cook. New York: Lawrence Hill Books, 1974.

The author presents historical, archaeological, and anthropological evidence to show that the civilization of ancient Egypt was produced by black Africans and that the Egyptians played a major role in the development of the classical civilizations of the Mediterranean.

———. *Civilization or Barbarism: An Authentic Anthropology.* Edited by Harold J. Salemson and Marjolijn De Jager. Translated by Yaa-Lengi Meema Ngemi. New York: Lawrence Hill Books, 1991.

Diop explores the historical achievements of Africans and the influence of African cultures on the development of civilization.

Drake, St. Clair. *Black Folk Here and There.* 2 vols. Los Angeles: University of California, Los Angeles, and the Center for Afro-American Studies, 1990.

The author uses an anthropological and historical framework to analyze the origins and development of color and race consciousness from ancient times to the rise of the slave trade.

Du Bois, W.E.B. *The World and Africa: An Inquiry into the Part Which Africa Has Played in World History.* Rev. ed. New York: International Publishing, 1965.

First published in 1947, this expanded edition includes Du Bois's writings on Africa from 1955 to 1961. In the wake of World War II, Du Bois criticized European colonialism and called on the colonial powers to relinquish the reins of government in Africa. The book includes recollections of the historic Pan-African conferences.

Harris, Joseph E. *Africans and Their History.* Rev. ed. New York: NAL-Dutton, Mentor, 1972.

This reevaluation of African cultures and politics reveals the ways in which African history has been distorted in the past and presents a concise overview of Africa's rich historical legacy.

Hay, Margaret Jean, and Sharon Stichter, eds. *African Women South of the Sahara.* White Plains, N.Y.: Longman, 1984.

This study examines the economic, social, and political roles of African women from precolonial days to the present.

Hull, Richard W. *African Cities and Towns before the European Conquest.* New York: Norton, 1977.

Urban life in precolonial Africa is the subject of this study, which examines the origins of African cities and towns and traces the development of urban life as it responded to the needs of changing populations. The author refutes the notion that modern African cities and towns were European creations, finding that African urban life has roots far deeper than nineteenth- and twentieth-century colonialism.

International Scientific Committee for the Drafting of a General History of Africa. *The UNESCO General History of Africa.* 7 vols. Berkeley: University of California Press, 1981–1992.

This ambitious series is a joint effort of the United Nations Educational, Scientific, and Cultural Organization (UNESCO) and the University of California Press. Its goal is to provide a scientific account of the ideas, civilizations, and traditions of the African peoples. The volumes are organized chronologically, each with a different author or editor. An eighth and final volume, covering the period from 1935 to the present, is forthcoming.

Jackson, John G. *Introduction to African Civilizations.* Secaucus, N.J.: Carol Publishing, Citadel Press, 1974.

This useful volume provides a general overview of African history and cultures from earliest times to the present.

Knight, Franklin W. *The Caribbean: The Genesis of a Fragmented Nationalism.* 2nd ed. New York: Oxford University Press, 1990.

This study offers an introduction to five centuries of life in the Caribbean.

Knight, Franklin W., and Colin A. Palmer, eds. *The Modern Caribbean.* Chapel Hill: University of North Carolina Press, 1989.

Thirteen essays written by experts in the field of Caribbean studies explore the diverse elements that have shaped the development of the modern Caribbean.

Kunene, Mazisi. *Emperor Shaka the Great.* Portsmouth, N.H.: Heinemann, 1979.

This verse narrative chronicles the life and achievements of the nineteenth-century Zulu leader who unified his people and attempted to coexist with English settlers. Critics have called this epic the literary—and African—equivalent of the *Iliad* and the *Odyssey.* The author has translated the work into English from the original Zulu.

Pakenham, Thomas. *The Scramble for Africa, 1876–1912.* New York: Random House, 1991.

European imperialism in Africa is the subject of this account, which traces the relentless movement of Europeans and Africans across the continent as they fought for control of the land. The author opens and closes the story with the Belgian king Leopold II, notorious for his brutality in the Congo (present-day Zaire). While focusing primarily on the motivations and actions of Europeans, the narrative provides a vivid sense of African life.

Rodney, Walter. *How Europe Underdeveloped Africa.* Washington, D.C.: Howard University Press, 1982.

The author focuses on the devastating effects of the slave trade and European colonialism on the development of African societies and the growth of African nations.

Romer, John. *Ancient Lives: Daily Life in the Egypt of the Pharaohs.* New York: Henry Holt, Owl Books, 1990.

Everyday life in ancient Egypt is the subject of this work, which is based on a fascinating array of archaeological evidence. A lively narrative describes the housing, clothing, food, festivals, and beliefs of ordinary Egyptians living in an extraordinary time.

Snowden, Frank. *Blacks in Antiquity: Ethiopians in the Greco-Roman Experience.* Cambridge, Mass.: Harvard University Press, Belknap Press, 1970.

The author explores attitudes toward Ethiopians—defined as all dark-skinned peoples of Africa—in the ancient world. He concludes that Ethiopians were accepted without prejudice of color and were highly regarded in a variety of roles, including that of diplomat, warrior, athlete, and performer. Exceptional illustrations of classical art depicting Africans in the ancient world complement the narrative.

————. *Before Color Prejudice: The Ancient View of Blacks.* Cambridge, Mass.: Harvard University Press, 1991.

Snowden expands his thesis that color prejudice did not exist in antiquity by examining a wider geographic area over a longer period of time. He finds that in the ancient world, color differences were not associated with inferiority or other prejudicial attitudes. The strong narrative and outstanding illustrations support the conclusion that racism is a post-classical innovation rather than a universal phenomenon.

Van Sertima, Ivan, ed. *Egypt Revisited.* 2nd ed. New Brunswick, N.J.: Transaction Publishers, 1989.

This collection of essays offers a new examination of ancient Egypt and its place as an African society. Topics covered include the race and origin of the ancient Egyptians, Egyptian dynasties and rulers, and Egyptian philosophy and science. Of special note for educators is Beatrice Lumpkin's "Ancient Egypt for Children—Facts, Fiction, and Lies."

Wallerstein, Immanuel. *Africa and the Modern World.* Trenton: Africa World Press, 1986.

Contemporary Africa and the development of its role in the world economy is the subject of this series of essays.

Williams, Chancellor. *The Destruction of Black Civilization: Great Issues of a Race from 4500 B.C. to 2000 A.D.* Rev. ed. Chicago: Third World Press, 1987.

This account of African history, which has both won acclaim and stirred controversy, examines the rise and fall of ancient African civilizations. The author challenges African Americans to reclaim their historic destiny as a great people.

United States History
Survey Texts, Reference Works, and General Overviews

Anderson, James D. *The Education of Blacks in the South, 1860–1935.* Chapel Hill: University of North Carolina Press, 1988.

Tracing the emergence of African-American schools in the South, the author explores the Hampton model of education, normal schools, common schools, and county training schools, as well as the ideological positions of liberal-arts education versus vocational education.

Aptheker, Herbert, ed. *A Documentary History of the Negro People in the United States.* 4 vols. New York: Carol Publishing, Citadel Press, 1989–1990.

This comprehensive series, first published from 1952 to 1975, is widely regarded as the definitive documentary history of black Americans. Aptheker uses a wealth of primary sources to chronicle the changing lives of African Americans during four periods in history. Volume 1 covers colonial times to the Civil War. Volume 2 covers Reconstruction to the founding of the National Association for the Advancement of Colored People (NAACP). Volume 3 covers 1910 to the beginning of the New Deal. Volume 4 covers the New Deal to the end of World War II.

Asante, Molefi K., and Mark T. Mattson. *Historical and Cultural Atlas of African Americans.* New York: Macmillan, 1991.

This reference provides a chronological survey of African-American history, a series of biographical portraits, and a statistical overview of African Americans today. The work includes 65 colorful and informative maps.

Bennett, Lerone. *The Shaping of Black America.* Chicago: Johnson Publishing, 1975.

This highly readable work offers an overview of the main themes in African-American history, emphasizing the origins of slavery and racism, the emancipation experience, and labor and business.

————. *Before the Mayflower: A History of Black America.* Rev. ed. New York: Viking Penguin, 1984.

Bennett traces the black experience from Africa to the United States in this eloquent general history. This edition contains an excellent chronology of events.

Berry, Mary Frances, and John W. Blassingame. *Long Memory: The Black Experience in America.* New York: Oxford University Press, 1982.

Autobiographies, newspapers, cartoons, songs, and poetry enhance this topical survey of African-American history. The work focuses on such themes as family and church, politics, economics, education, criminal justice, and black nationalism.

Billingsley, Andrew. *Black Families in White America.* Rev. ed. New York: Simon & Schuster, Touchstone Books, 1988.

First published in 1969, this work analyzes the history, structures, aspirations, and problems of African-American families.

Bond, Horace Mann. *The Education of the Negro in the American Social Order.* New York: Octagon Books, 1966.

Useful background information describing the factors that have impacted African-American education is provided in this study, which was originally published in 1934.

Brotz, Howard, ed. *African-American Social and Political Thought, 1850–1920.* New Brunswick, N.J.: Transaction Publishers, 1991.

This collection presents the writings of Frederick Douglass, W.E.B. Du Bois, Booker T. Washington, Marcus Garvey, and others as they addressed the social and political questions of their day. Each author offered plans of action that ranged from accommodation to emigration.

Cantor, George. *Historic Landmarks of Black America.* Detroit: Gale Research, 1991.

This illustrated guide highlights some 300 sites that are significant to African-American history, including historic houses, museums, libraries, churches, colleges, memorials, forts, and battlefields. The guide is organized by region, and each entry includes a description of the importance of the site as well as its location, hours of operation, admission charge (if any), and telephone number.

Du Bois, W.E.B. *The Education of Black People: Ten Critiques, 1906–1960.* Edited by Herbert Aptheker. New York: Monthly Review, 1975.

Ten essays and speeches, created during a 50-year period, chronicle Du Bois's tireless efforts for excellence in higher education for African Americans.

Foner, Philip S., and Ronald L. Lewis, eds. *Black Workers Selections: A Documentary History from Colonial Times to the Present.* Philadelphia: Temple University Press, 1988.

This collection of primary sources provides an overview of the experiences of African-American workers throughout our nation's history.

Forbes, Jack. *Black Africans and Native Americans.* Cambridge, Mass.: Basil Blackwell, 1988.

This study explores the contacts and relations between Africans and Native Americans from pre-Columbian times to the nineteenth century. The work provides valuable insights into the development of modern American culture and the evolution of race relations in the Western Hemisphere.

Franklin, John Hope, and Alfred A. Moss., Jr. *From Slavery to Freedom: A History of Negro Americans.* 6th ed. New York: Alfred A. Knopf, 1988.

This comprehensive work, first published in 1948, is a classic in the field. In this updated edition, the authors explore the African-American experience from the heritage of Ghana, Mali, and Songhai to modern American society.

Frederickson, George M. *The Black Image in the White Mind: The Debate on Afro-American Character and Destiny, 1817–1914.* Hanover, N.H.: University Press of New England, 1987.

The author traces the changing ideas about African Americans held by various segments of the European-American population from the early nineteenth century to World War I. The work explores the rationalizations and pseudoscientific ideology that helped shape American racial attitudes.

Giddings, Paula. *When and Where I Enter: The Impact of Black Women on Race and Sex in America.* New York: Bantam, 1985.

This engaging narrative focuses on the experiences of African-American women in the United States in the late nineteenth and the twentieth centuries.

Hine, Darlene C., ed. *The State of Afro-American History: Past, Present, and Future.* Baton Rouge: Louisiana State University Press, 1986.

This collection of essays on African-American history features such scholars as John Hope Franklin, Thomas Holt, William Harris, Nathan Huggins, Vincent Harding, and the editor of this volume. A critique follows each essay.

Hornsby, Alton, Jr., ed. *Chronology of African-American History: Significant Events and People from 1619 to the Present.* Detroit: Gale Research, 1991.

This reference lists births and deaths, laws and court decisions, rebellions and demonstrations, honors and awards, elections and appointments, and other data important to African-American history. The entries are arranged chronologically. The work also includes brief biographies of noteworthy individuals as well as excerpts from significant documents.

Hughes, Langston, and Milton Meltzer. *African-American History.* New York: Scholastic, 1990.

Originally published under the title *A Pictorial History of the Negro in America,* this important work provides a wealth of information about the black experience from the heritage of Africa to the contributions of African Americans today.

Ione, Carole. *Pride of Family: Four Generations of American Women of Color.* New York: Summit Books, 1991.

The lives of four generations of women in the author's family are chronicled in this account, which focuses on each woman's search for identity and independence. The work provides a history of black women's experiences as well as a social history of the times in which they lived. One fascinating primary source the author uses is her great-grandmother's diary, which offers personal insights into the hopes and disappointments of Reconstruction.

James, Portia. *The Real McCoy: African-American Invention and Innovation, 1619–1930.* Washington, D.C.: Smithsonian Institution Press, 1989.

This valuable guide surveys the achievements of African-American inventors during more than 300 years of American history. The book includes a wide variety of inventions that contributed to American technology, including the "Real McCoy"—a locomotive lubricating device invented by African American Elijah McCoy.

Jones, Jacqueline. *Labor of Love, Labor of Sorrow: Black Women, Work, and the Family from Slavery to the Present.* New York: Random House, Vintage, 1986.

This book provides a vivid and sensitive social and historical account of how African-American women have worked and lived.

Jones-Jackson, Patricia. *When Roots Die: Endangered Traditions on the Sea Islands.* Athens: University of Georgia Press, 1989.

The author describes Gullah language, lore, and traditions and appeals for ways to preserve this unique culture in the wake of increasing development on the sea islands.

Katz, William L. *Black Indians: A Hidden Heritage.* New York: Macmillan, Atheneum, 1986.

The author uses rare antique prints to help tell the story of how African Americans and Native Americans coexisted in several Native-American nations, joining forces against the oppression imposed on them by European Americans.

Lincoln, C. Eric. *Race, Religion, and the Continuing American Dilemma.* New York: Hill & Wang, 1984.

The author traces the history of African-American religion from the eighteenth century to modern times, highlighting religion and black ethnicity, identity, and nationalism.

Lincoln, C. Eric, and Lawrence H. Mamiya. *The Black Church in the African-American Experience.* Durham: Duke University Press, 1990.

Drawing on data obtained from interviews with members of the clergy, as well as on an overview of seven black denominations, this field study offers an analysis of the role of the church in African-American history and in contemporary culture.

Logan, Rayford W., and Michael R. Winston. *Dictionary of American Negro Biography.* New York: Norton, 1983.

Biographical sketches of more than 200 outstanding African Americans from many different walks of life are contained in this indispensable reference book.

Low, Augustus W., and Virgil A. Clift, eds. *Encyclopedia of Black America.* New York: Da Capo Press, 1984.

This reference provides a wide range of data about African-American life, past and present.

Major, Geri. *Black Society.* Chicago: Johnson Publishing, 1977.

The author traces the evolution of free black society—its leaders, values, and challenges—from the colonial period to the present.

Malson, Micheline, et al., eds. *Black Women in America: Social Science Perspectives.* Chicago: University of Chicago Press, 1990.

This collection of essays focuses on the experiences of African-American women, exploring such topics as family roles, job satisfaction, economic status, and traditions in the church.

Nalty, Bernard C. *Strength for the Fight: A History of Black Americans in the Military.* New York: Free Press, 1989.

African Americans have served courageously in the military from colonial days to the present, despite the difficulties of fighting racial prejudice as well as the country's enemies. This informative book effectively examines this sensitive subject.

Ploski, Harry A., and James Williams, eds. *The Negro Almanac: A Reference Work on the African American.* 6th ed. Detroit: Gale Research, 1992.

This comprehensive volume offers a wide range of information on the history and culture of African Americans. The book is organized by subject and includes such chapters as The Black Voter and Elected Officeholder and The Black Family. Each chapter is supported by significant documents, chronological summaries, biographical profiles, statistics, and illustrations.

Quarles, Benjamin. *The Negro in the Making of America.* New York: Macmillan, 1987.

African-American history from the origins of European slaving to the American civil rights movement is chronicled in this highly acclaimed work. Originally published in 1964, this insightful study documents the struggles and achievements of African Americans as they have helped shape life in the United States.

Shapiro, Herbert. *White Violence and Black Response: From Reconstruction to Montgomery.* Amherst: University of Massachusetts Press, 1988.

In this penetrating study the author examines selected violent events perpetrated against African Americans, the failure of the nation's legal system to halt the violence, and how the black community responded.

Smith, Edward D. *Climbing Jacob's Ladder: The Rise of Black Churches in Eastern American Cities, 1740–1877.* Washington, D.C.: Smithsonian Institution Press, 1988.

This book traces the vital role early churches played in the development of African-American communities on the East Coast. The author underscores the notion that before there can be an African-American community, there must be an African-American church.

Sterling, Dorothy, ed. *We Are Your Sisters: Black Women in the Nineteenth Century.* New York: Norton, 1985.

The daily lives of African-American women in the nineteenth century are reflected in this collection of speeches, petitions, and other primary sources. The documents address a wide range of topics concerning both enslaved and free women, including childhood experiences, work, courtship, and family life.

Stewart, Paul W., and Wallace Y. Ponce. *Black Cowboys.* Broomfield, Colo.: Phillips Publishing, 1986.

This book highlights the experiences of the African-American pioneers who moved to the Western frontier and contributed to its growth. The book contains many rare photographs that were once part of exhibits at the Black American West Museum in Denver, Colorado.

Turner, William H., and Edward J. Cabell, eds. *Blacks in Appalachia.* Lexington: University Press of Kentucky, 1985.

This collection offers the first comprehensive presentation of the black experience in Appalachia.

Van Sertima, Ivan. *They Came before Columbus: The African Presence in Ancient America.* New York: Random House, Vintage, 1989.

In this controversial book the author presents evidence to show that Africans came to North and South America centuries before Christopher Columbus.

Wilson, Charles R., and William Ferris, eds. *Encyclopedia of Southern Culture.* Chapel Hill: University of North Carolina Press, 1989.

This comprehensive volume offers an intriguing portrait of the diverse and distinctive culture of the American South. The work is organized according to 24 thematic sections, including a section on black life.

Woodson, Carter G. *The Miseducation of the Negro.* Trenton: Africa World Press, 1990.

Written in 1933, this book contains the philosophical basis for Woodson's lifelong commitment to African-American education. Among the first to link curriculum reform to self-esteem and achievement, Woodson criticized educators for overlooking the history and culture of Africa and African Americans and argued for a thorough revamping of the American educational system.

Woodson, Carter G., and Charles H. Wesley. *The Negro in Our History.* 11th ed. Washington, D.C.: Associated Publishers, 1966.

Originally published in 1922 and repeatedly enlarged and revised, this history of Africans and African Americans was designed for both the student and the general reader. Although it has since been supplanted by other works, *The Negro in Our History* was considered the outstanding textbook in the field for many years. One adaptation of the book was Woodson's *The Story of the Negro Retold* (1935).

Slavery and Abolition

Aptheker, Herbert. *American Negro Slave Revolts.* 5th ed. New York: International Publishing, 1983.

This pioneering work documents the courage and determination of those who took direct action to free themselves from the horrors of slavery.

Bell, Malcolm. *Major Butler's Legacy: Five Generations of a Slaveholding Family.* Athens: University of Georgia Press, 1987.

This portrait of one family's agricultural empire provides valuable insights into the plantation system. The book offers rich detail about the daily lives of family members as well as those of the slaves who worked their lands. Bell makes extensive use of primary sources such as family correspondence, diaries, and slave inventories, along with records of black births, deaths, escapes, and punishments.

Berlin, Ira, and Ronald Hoffman, eds. *Slavery and Freedom in the Age of the American Revolution.* Champaign: University of Illinois Press, 1986.

This series of essays focuses on the changing patterns of slavery and free black society during the revolutionary period. The work also examines current developments in the study of slavery in the United States.

Blassingame, John W. *The Slave Community: Plantation Life in the Antebellum South.* 2nd ed. New York: Oxford University Press, 1979.

Blassingame uses an interdisciplinary approach to explore plantation life in the prewar South from the point of view of the people held as slaves. Much of the work deals with the effects of oppression on those enslaved.

Blockson, Charles L. *The Underground Railroad: First-Person Narratives of Escapes to Freedom in the North.* Englewood Cliffs, N.J.: Prentice-Hall, 1987.

This book provides a state-by-state description of the activities of the Underground Railroad during the antebellum period.

Brandt, Nat. *The Town That Started the Civil War.* New York: Dell, 1991.

The author examines antislavery activities in the Western Reserve, a large tract of land in Ohio that included the town of Oberlin. The focus of the study is an 1858 incident in which townspeople rescued a kidnapped fugitive slave and were jailed for violating fugitive-slave laws. The events that followed heightened antislavery sentiment in the area.

Campbell, Edward D.C., Jr., ed. *Before Freedom Came: African-American Life in the Antebellum South.* With Kym S. Rice. Charlottesville: University Press of Virginia, 1991.

Published to accompany an exhibition organized by the Museum of the Confederacy, this richly illustrated book surveys the experiences of enslaved African Americans in the antebellum South. Six essays written by noted scholars include Slavery in the American Experience, Plantation Landscapes of the Antebellum South, The World of the Plantation Slaves, Female Slaves in the Plantation South, Black Life in Old South Cities, and Archaeology of Slave Life.

Creel, Margaret W. *A Peculiar People: Slave Religion and Community Culture among the Gullah.* New York: New York University Press, 1989.

The subject of this fascinating study is the development of the unique culture of the Gullah people of South Carolina's sea islands during the eighteenth and nineteenth centuries. The author explores the ways in which the Gullahs, though enslaved, resisted white cultural domination by building their own "peculiar" community.

Davis, David B. *Slavery and Human Progress.* New York: Oxford University Press, 1986.

The connections between slavery and the idea of progress are explored in this important work. The study provides penetrating insights into slavery and emancipation throughout world history and includes current debates on new forms of forced labor.

Ferguson, Leland. *Uncommon Ground: Archaeology and Colonial African America.* Washington, D.C.: Smithsonian Institution Press, 1991.

By piecing together new evidence from recent archaeological studies, the author of this fascinating and provocative work offers a vivid picture of the culture of early African-American slaves—as distinct from the culture of European Americans—in the years before the American Revolution.

Fox-Genovese, Elizabeth. *Within the Plantation Household: Black and White Women of the Old South.* Chapel Hill: University of North Carolina Press, 1988.

This insightful work examines plantation households in terms of the relationships between mistresses and bondswomen. The author dispels the notion that there was bonding between the groups because of gender, contending instead that the plantation mistresses supported the system that made it possible for them to lead privileged lives.

Gutman, Herbert G. *The Black Family in Slavery and Freedom, 1750–1925.* New York: Random House, Vintage, 1977.

In this major work, the author shows that slavery and poverty did not shatter African-American family ties, as some have argued.

Harding, Vincent. *There Is a River: The Black Struggle for Freedom in America.* New York: Random House, Vintage, 1982.

This powerful account presents the black struggle against slavery from the early days of rebellion on the slave ships docked off the coast of West Africa to the resistance of daring escapes, secret publications, illegal schools, civil disobedience, and violence that finally led to war and emancipation.

James, Howard. *Mutiny on the* Amistad: *The Saga of a Slave Revolt and Its Impact on American Abolition, Law, and Diplomacy.* New York: Oxford University Press, 1987.

The 1839 slave revolt aboard the Spanish slave ship *Amistad* created an international controversy over the issue of slavery.

Jordan, Winthrop D. *White over Black: American Attitudes toward the Negro, 1550–1812.* New York: Norton, 1977.

The author explores the development of racial attitudes toward African Americans during the early years of American history, providing insights as to the origins of racial stereotypes as well as important background information for an understanding of the long struggle for civil rights.

Joyner, Charles. *Down by the Riverside: A South Carolina Slave Community.* Champaign: University of Illinois Press, 1984.

This book examines the day-to-day lives of slaves in the rice-growing region of South Carolina—what they ate, how they dressed, and how they celebrated and mourned.

Kaminski, John P., and Richard Leffler, eds. *A Necessary Evil? Slavery and the Debate over the Constitution.* Madison, Wis.: Madison House, 1991.

The slavery issue as debated by members of the Constitutional Convention is the subject of this study.

Kemble, Frances Anne. *Journal of a Residence on a Georgian Plantation in 1838–1839.* Edited by John A. Scott. Athens: University of Georgia Press, 1984.

In the 1830s a British actress named Fanny Kemble married a wealthy Philadelphian, Pierce Butler, during her American tour. After her marriage she was shocked to discover the source of his wealth—a Georgia sea island plantation with 700 slaves. The entries in Kemble's journal offer a frank, firsthand account of life and living conditions on the plantation for both owners and slaves.

Kulikoff, Allan. *Tobacco and Slaves: The Development of Southern Culture in the Chesapeake, 1680–1800.* Chapel Hill: University of North Carolina Press, 1986.

This history of the Chesapeake examines the political and economic transformation that tobacco brought to the region and the effects these changes had on both African Americans and European Americans.

Littlefield, Daniel C. *Rice and Slaves: Ethnicity and the Slave Trade in Colonial South Carolina.* Champaign: University of Illinois Press, 1991.

This study focuses on the impact enslaved Africans had on the development of colonial South Carolina, especially in terms of agriculture and the cultivation of rice.

Mellon, James, ed.   *Bullwhip Days: The Slaves Remember.*   New York: Avon, 1990.

Compiled from hundreds of interviews with former slaves conducted by the Federal Writers' Project during the 1930s, this absorbing collection of personal stories provides an invaluable social history of life under slavery. The work includes 29 narrative oral histories as well as 9 sections of excerpts related to particular aspects of slave life.

Nash, Gary B.   *Red, White, and Black: The Peoples of Early America.*   2nd ed. Englewood Cliffs, N.J.: Prentice-Hall, 1982.

In this informative history of early America, the author examines the various segments of colonial society, including those whose labor and land were exploited in attempts to fulfill the promise of colonial society.

————.   *Race and Revolution.*   Madison, Wis.: Madison House, 1990.

This study describes how members of the African-American community in the North responded to the failure to include them in the American Dream following the American Revolution.

Owens, Leslie Howard.   *This Species of Property: Slave Life and Culture in the Old South.*   New York: Oxford University Press, 1976.

The author describes daily life among those held as slaves in the American South, focusing on the importance of the slave community as a source of values, customs, traditions, and beliefs. The study gives new attention to the effects of malnutrition and disease on the slave population.

Pease, Jane H., and William H. Pease.   *They Who Would Be Free: Blacks' Search for Freedom, 1830–1861.*   Champaign: University of Illinois Press, 1990.

This book explores the differences that divided black and white abolitionists in the years leading to the Civil War—differences concerning not only the best means to acquire freedom for African Americans but also the definition of freedom itself.

Sobel, Mechal. *The World They Made Together: Black and White Values in Eighteenth-Century Virginia.* Princeton: Princeton University Press, 1989.

In this study the author discusses the ways in which African Americans and European Americans influenced the development of society in the eighteenth-century South. Both groups helped form new cultural values in terms of ideas about work, time, space, causality, purpose, and the natural world.

Stuckey, Sterling. *Slave Culture: Nationalist Theory and the Foundations of Black America.* New York: Oxford University Press, 1988.

The author illustrates how enslaved Africans from many different ethnic groups shared a value system that enabled them to achieve a common culture in the United States. This culture created a sense of nationalism that gave African Americans identity and an ideological foundation, as reflected in the works of such intellectuals as David Walker, Martin Delaney, W.E.B. Du Bois, and Paul Robeson. Historical data for this work were gathered through extensive anthropological studies of West African cultural traditions.

Swift, David E. *Black Prophets of Justice: Activist Clergy before the Civil War.* Baton Rouge: Louisiana State University Press, 1989.

This study focuses on the work of six African-American church leaders who fought tirelessly against the racism of their day. The six profiled are Samuel Cornish, Theodore Wright, Charles Ray, Henry Highland Garnet, Amos Beman, and James Pennington.

Turner, Nat. *The Confessions of Nat Turner, Leader of the Late Insurrection in Southampton, Va., As Fully and Voluntarily Made to Thos. C. Gray.* Salem, N.H.: Ayer, 1969.

Turner's statement as made in prison and acknowledged by him at his 1831 trial is presented in this facsimile edition.

Walker, David. *David Walker's Appeal.* Edited by Charles Wiltse. New York: Hill & Wang, 1965.

This fiery condemnation of racism and slavery, written in 1829 by the African-American abolitionist David Walker, sparked the radical antislavery movement in the United States. Walker's strident call for enslaved Americans to fight for their freedom brought dread to slaveholders, who feared widespread uprisings, and dismay to pacifist abolitionists, who preached against the spiraling effects of violence.

Free Blacks

Alexander, Adele Logan. *Ambiguous Lives: Free Women of Color in Rural Georgia, 1789–1879.* Fayetteville: University of Arkansas Press, 1991.

The lives of free women of mixed race in the rural South during the era of slavery, the Civil War, and Reconstruction are explored in this study, in which the author profiles members of her own family as representative of this segment of the African-American community.

Curry, Leonard P. *The Free Black in Urban America, 1800–1850: The Shadow of the Dream.* Chicago: University of Chicago Press, 1986.

This work examines the free black communities that developed in the 15 largest cities of the antebellum United States. While recognizing the rich diversity that existed among the communities, the author points to the patterns of racial discrimination that influenced the black urban experience throughout the country.

Foner, Philip S., and George F. Walker, eds. *Proceedings of Black State Conventions, 1840–1865.* 2 vols. Philadelphia: Temple University Press, 1979.

These volumes offer a rare compilation of the proceedings of black state conventions held during the years leading to the Civil War. Most often called to redress wrongs perpetrated upon free black people, such conventions also dealt with the subject of slavery.

Horton, James O., and Lois E. Horton. *Black Bostonians: Family Life and Community Struggle in the Antebellum North.* New York: Holmes and Meier, 1979.

Everyday life in Boston's black community during the years before the Civil War is the focus of this fascinating book. The profile of this vital community reveals the world of free African Americans in the urban North and the network of family and community ties that helped them survive.

Johnson, Michael P., and James L. Roark. *Black Masters: A Free Family of Color in the Old South.* New York: Norton, 1986.

William Ellison was a former slave who became "a free man of color." Skilled at repairing and building cotton gins, Ellison eventually became quite wealthy, owning his own plantation and slaves. The authors use a wide range of primary sources to piece together the unique story of Ellison and his family.

Piersen, William D. *Black Yankees: The Development of an Afro-American Subculture in Eighteenth-Century New England.* Amherst: University of Massachusetts Press, 1988.

This book focuses on the African-American enclaves that developed in Rhode Island, Connecticut, and Massachusetts during the eighteenth century.

Putney, Martha S. *Black Sailors: Afro-American Merchant Seamen and Whalemen prior to the Civil War.* Westport, Conn.: Greenwood Press, 1987.

This history of African-American sailors is based on an examination of crew lists, ship manifests, registers, and protection papers, as well as on data from the Bureau of Customs.

The Civil War and Reconstruction

Berlin, Ira, et al., eds. *Freedom: A Documentary History of Emancipation, 1861–1867.* 3 vols. New York: Cambridge University Press, 1983–1991.

This series presents a superb collection of primary sources, selected from the holdings of the National Archives, on slavery and the process of freedom in the United States. The three titles available in what is projected to be a five-volume series are *The Destruction of Slavery, The Black Military Experience,* and *The Wartime Genesis of Free Labor: The Lower South.*

Bethel, Elizabeth R. *Promiseland: A Century of Life in a Negro Community.* Philadelphia: Temple University Press, 1982.

This engaging study focuses on the community of Promiseland, a product of South Carolina's effort to distribute lands to freed slaves during Reconstruction. The unique experience of the town's residents helped forge the ties that held the community together through difficult times.

Cornish, Dudley T. *The Sable Arm: Black Troops in the Union Army, 1861–1865.* Lawrence: University Press of Kansas, 1987.

First published in 1956, this book illustrates the vital role played by African-American troops during the Civil War.

Cox, LaWanda. *Lincoln and Black Freedom: A Study in Presidential Leadership.* Champaign: University of Illinois Press, 1985.

Using an analysis of presidential policy in wartime Louisiana as a case study, the author examines Abraham Lincoln's leadership style as he worked toward a solution to the divisive issue of slavery.

Drago, Edmund L. *Black Politicians and Reconstruction in Georgia: A Splendid Failure.* Baton Rouge: Louisiana State University Press, 1982.

This account details the process of Reconstruction as it took place in Georgia, focusing on black leadership in the years following the Civil War.

Du Bois, W.E.B. *Black Reconstruction.* Millwood, N.Y.: Kraus International, 1976.

When originally published in 1935, this work was labeled revisionist for its overall positive view of the role played by African Americans during Reconstruction. Du Bois applauds much of the work of the Reconstruction state legislatures and conventions and stresses that economic factors and the revolt of black workers were decisive in precipitating the Civil War and the ultimate Union victory.

Foner, Eric. *Reconstruction: America's Unfinished Revolution, 1863–1877.* New York: Harper & Row, 1989.

This lively narrative offers a fresh perspective on how African Americans and European Americans responded to the unique opportunity of reconstructing the country after the Civil War.

Glatthaar, Joseph T. *Forged in Battle: The Civil War Alliance of Black Soldiers and White Officers.* New York: NAL-Dutton, Meridian Books, 1991.

During the Civil War more than 7,000 white officers commanded almost 180,000 black soldiers. This study, based on personal letters and official documents, explores the relationship between the two groups.

Hermann, Janet S. *The Pursuit of a Dream.* New York: Oxford University Press, 1981.

This book traces the history of an experimental black community in Mississippi during a period from the 1820s to the 1920s. First planned as a model slave plantation, the community was rebuilt by African Americans during Reconstruction. At the heart of the story are two Southern families—one white, one black—and how each worked to fulfill the dream of utopian living.

Litwack, Leon F. *Been in the Storm So Long: The Aftermath of Slavery.* New York: Random House, Vintage, 1980.

The author skillfully examines the dramatic and complex changes that took place in the United States in the years immediately following emancipation.

Long, Richard A., ed. *Black Writers and the American Civil War.* Secaucus, N.J.: Book Sales, 1989.

The writings of African Americans before and during the Civil War are highlighted in this collection. Recorded are the experiences, observations, and concerns of people such as William Wells Brown, George Washington Williams, Joseph T. Wilson, Susie King Taylor, Charlotte Forten, Francis Allen, and Frederick Douglass.

McPherson, James M. *Battle Cry of Freedom: The Civil War Era.* New York: Ballantine, 1989.

McPherson provides a compelling, highly readable account of the political, economic, military, and social factors that shaped the Civil War era.

Pease, William H., and Jane H. Pease. *Black Utopia: Negro Communal Experiments in America.* Madison: State Historical Society of Wisconsin, 1972.

This book is an important study of the attempts to establish model communities in the United States and Canada for emancipated African Americans. The Port Royal experiment is one example of this effort.

Rabinowitz, Howard N., ed. *Southern Black Leaders of the Reconstruction Era.* Champaign: University of Illinois Press, 1982.

A wealth of information is provided in this series of essays about the African-American leaders of the South in the years following the Civil War.

Walker, Clarence E. *A Rock in a Weary Land: The African Methodist Episcopal Church during the Civil War and Reconstruction.* Baton Rouge: Louisiana State University Press, 1982.

The role of the African Methodist Episcopal Church as it grappled with the issues surrounding emancipation and Reconstruction is the subject of this book.

Wayne, Michael. *The Reshaping of Plantation Society: The Natchez District, 1860–1880.* Champaign: University of Illinois Press, 1990.

The changing relationship between planters and emancipated African Americans during the Civil War and Reconstruction are described in this study.

Life at the Turn of the Century

Cohen, William. *At Freedom's Edge: Black Mobility and the Southern White Quest for Racial Control, 1861–1915.* Baton Rouge: Louisiana State University Press, 1991.

This study presents a comprehensive history of black mobility from the Civil War to World War I, giving special attention to the South. The author treats mobility as a central component of black freedom that influenced the emergence of a free labor system and helped to block attempts by Southern leaders to control the lives of African Americans.

Cox, Thomas C. *Blacks in Topeka, Kansas, 1865–1915: A Social History.* Baton Rouge: Louisiana State University Press, 1982.

The author chronicles the social, political, and economic development of the African-American community in Topeka, Kansas, in the years following the Civil War.

De Vries, James E. *Race and Kinship in a Midwestern Town: The Black Experience in Monroe, Michigan, 1900–1915.* Champaign: University of Illinois Press, 1984.

This historical account examines the lives of African Americans living, working, and adjusting to life in a small Midwestern town.

Du Bois, W.E.B. *The Souls of Black Folk.* New York: Random House, 1990.

Regarded as Du Bois's greatest work, this collection of essays blends memoir, history, sociology, biography, and fiction. It was in this book that Du Bois first publicly distanced himself from the accommodationist tactics of Booker T. Washington and gained national recognition as Washington's ideological rival.

Gatewood, Willard. *Aristocrats of Color: The Black Elite, 1880–1920.* Bloomington: Indiana University Press, 1990.

Gatewood offers a valuable study of the social structure of African-American communities of the late nineteenth and early twentieth centuries. The author bases his conclusions on an analysis of caste, class, and color.

Hamilton, Kenneth Marvin. *Black Towns and Profit: Promotion and Development in the Trans-Appalachian West, 1877–1915.* Champaign: University of Illinois Press, 1991.

The author explores the origins and early development of five black towns on the expanding Western frontier—Nicodemus, Kansas; Mound Bayou, Mississippi; Langston City, Oklahoma; Boley, Oklahoma; and Allensworth, California.

McDaniel, George W. *Hearth and Home: Preserving a People's Culture.* Philadelphia: Temple University Press, 1984.

To tell the story of the everyday life of rural African Americans in the nineteenth century, the author combines a study of material culture and social history.

Moss, Alfred A., Jr. *The American Negro Academy: Voice of the Talented Tenth.* Baton Rouge: Louisiana State University Press, 1981.

This work focuses on the American Negro Academy—the first major African-American learned society. The study emphasizes the academy's mission of promoting intellectual growth and refuting racism. The book assesses the leadership of W.E.B. Du Bois, William Crogman, Alexander Crummell, and Francis J. Grimke.

Neverdon-Morton, Cynthia. *Afro-American Women of the South and the Advancement of the Race, 1895–1925.* Knoxville: University of Tennessee Press, 1989.

The turn of the century witnessed a steady increase in the number of African-American women in the South attending college, where they were inspired with the missionary zeal to make contributions to black society. Many of these women, in turn, inspired others to carry on their legacy.

Rachleff, Peter J. *Black Labor in Richmond, 1865–1890.* Champaign: University of Illinois Press, 1989.

Black labor in Richmond is the focus of this analysis, which provides insights into the experiences of African-American workers throughout the South during Reconstruction.

Woodward, C. Vann. *The Strange Career of Jim Crow.* 3rd ed. New York: Oxford University Press, 1974.

The author's classic study examines the development of the system of laws and practices that supported racial segregation in the late eighteenth and early nineteenth centuries.

The Twentieth Century

Allen, Robert L. *The Port Chicago Mutiny.* New York: Warner Books, 1989.

In 1944 a terrible explosion at the ammunition depot at Port Chicago, California, claimed 320 lives. Charging that they were being singled out to work under unsafe conditions, 50 African-American sailors refused to continue to load ammunition at the depot. The military subsequently charged them with mutiny. The story of their trial drew national attention to the policy of segregation in the armed forces.

Arnold, Thomas St. John. *Buffalo Soldiers: The 92nd Infantry Division and Reinforcements in World War II, 1942–1945.* Manhattan, Kans.: Sunflower University Press, 1990.

A former officer tells the story of the 92nd, the largest African-American division to see action in World War II.

Comer, James P. *Maggie's American Dream: The Life and Times of a Black Family.* New York: NAL-Dutton, 1989.

This poignant book chronicles the life of a remarkable woman— the author's mother, Maggie, who faced extraordinary challenges yet managed to propel her five children to earn 13 college degrees. After presenting his mother's story, the author focuses on his own story as he made his way through college and medical school in the 1940s and 1950s. Comer, a professor of child psychiatry, credits his family's success to his mother's belief in the value of education.

Cortner, Richard C. *A Mob Intent on Death: The NAACP and the Arkansas Riot Cases.* Middletown, Conn.: University Press of New England, Wesleyan University Press, 1988.

A 1919 racial confrontation between white planters and black sharecroppers in the village of Hoop Spur, Arkansas, is the focus of this study. More than 25 people, most of whom were black, were killed. The state called it a planned insurrection and sentenced 12 African Americans to death and 67 others to prison. The book tells the story of the NAACP attorneys who worked tirelessly to prove the innocence of those accused and finally won their freedom.

Daniel, Pete. *The Shadow of Slavery: Peonage in the South, 1901–1969.* 2nd ed. Champaign: University of Illinois Press, 1990.

This updated study on peonage in the South includes new material on peonage cases that have reached the courts in the last 20 years.

Fine, Sidney. *Violence in the Model City: The Cavanaugh Administration, Race Relations, and the Detroit Riot of 1967.* Ann Arbor: University of Michigan Press, 1989.

Eyewitness interviews and a variety of other primary sources are used to analyze the forces that sparked the 1967 rebellion in Detroit.

Harris, William. *Keeping the Faith: A. Philip Randolph, Milton P. Webster, and the Brotherhood of Sleeping Car Porters, 1925–1937.* Champaign: University of Illinois Press, 1991.

This study offers valuable insights into the role of black workers in the American labor movement, focusing on the union of Pullman car porters.

Lay, Shawn, ed. *The Invisible Empire in the West: Toward a New Historical Appraisal of the Ku Klux Klan of the 1920s.* Champaign: University of Illinois Press, 1991.

New views on the rise of the Ku Klux Klan during the early twentieth century are offered in this anthology.

Lemann, Nicholas. *The Promised Land: The Great Black Migration and How It Changed America.* New York: Alfred A. Knopf, 1991.

The cities of Clarksdale, Mississippi, and Chicago, Illinois, serve as case studies in this absorbing narrative, which describes the movement of African Americans from South to North in the years following World War I. The author emphasizes the effects of the migration on individual lives, interweaving the personal stories of African Americans and their families with the sweep of events throughout the nation up to the present day.

McMillen, Neil R. *Dark Journey: Black Mississippians in the Age of Jim Crow.* Champaign: University of Illinois Press, 1989.

Life for African Americans in Mississippi during the age of Jim Crow segregation is the focus of this book.

Meier, August, and Elliott Rudwick. *Black Detroit and the Rise of the UAW.* New York: Oxford University Press, 1979.

This in-depth study examines the interaction among the United Automobile Workers, the black community, and the federal bureaucracy that forged an alliance between black activism and industrial unionism during the 1930s and 1940s.

Schall, Keith L. *Stony Road: Chapters in the History of Hampton Institute.* Charlottesville: University Press of Virginia, 1977.

The essays in this collection describe the rich legacy of Hampton Institute in Virginia, one of the foremost African-American colleges.

Taulbert, Clifton L. *Once Upon a Time When We Were Colored.* Tulsa: Council Oak Books, 1991.

The town of Glen Allan, Mississippi, is the setting for this moving memoir about growing up in the waning days of enforced segregation. The author's heartwarming recollections tell the story of the loving family and supportive community that shaped his life in the segregated environment of the rural South.

Trotter, Joe William, Jr. *Coal, Class, and Color: Blacks in Southern West Virginia, 1915–1932.* Champaign: University of Illinois Press, 1990.

Trotter focuses on the black communities that developed in West Virginia coal towns in the early twentieth century. Unlike the African Americans who migrated to the cities, those who worked in the coal fields experienced the changes brought by industrialization without urbanization.

Washburn, Patrick S. *A Question of Sedition: The Federal Government's Investigation of the Black Press during World War II.* New York: Oxford University Press, 1986.

Set during World War II, this book examines attempts to censor the black press, which was calling for freedom for African Americans at home as well as for victory overseas.

The Civil Rights Movement

Branch, Taylor. *Parting the Waters: America in the King Years, 1954–1963.* New York: Simon & Schuster, Touchstone Books, 1989.

The fears, frustration, and excitement of the civil rights struggle are brought to life in this work, which offers compelling portraits of the individuals whose courage changed the course of American history. The study focuses on Dr. Martin Luther King, Jr., giving special attention to his role as a moral and religious leader.

Carson, Clayborne. *In Struggle: SNCC and the Black Awakening of the 1960s.* Cambridge, Mass.: Harvard University Press, 1981.

The author traces the development of the Student Nonviolent Coordinating Committee from the optimism of its founding in the early 1960s, through the period of disillusionment and more intense community action, to the black power movement at the end of the decade.

Carson, Clayborne, Ralph E. Luker, and Penny A. Russell, eds. *The Papers of Martin Luther King, Jr.: Called to Serve, January 1929–June 1951.* Vol. 1. Berkeley: University of California Press, 1992.

The first volume in a projected 14-volume series, *Called to Serve* chronicles King's early years. The work includes a wide variety of previously unpublished documents, such as letters, student essays and exams, and family photographs. The Martin Luther King, Jr., Papers Project at Stanford University was established by the King Center in Atlanta. The entire series is expected to be published over the next 20 years.

Forman, James. *The Making of Black Revolutionaries: A Personal Account.* 2nd ed. Seattle: Open Hand, 1985.

This memoir focuses on the author's experiences as a civil rights activist in the South and as a leader of the Student Nonviolent Coordinating Committee (SNCC) during the 1960s. Forman draws upon his own diary and notes as well as on primary sources from other civil rights workers to present a moving, personal account of the turmoil of the period.

Graham, Hugh D. *The Civil Rights Era: Origins and Development of National Policy, 1960–1972.* New York: Oxford University Press, 1990.

One aspect of the civil rights struggle that many people have forgotten is the debate that occurred in Congress and the White House. This study, which is based on extensive archival research, focuses on that debate.

Hampton, Henry, and Steve Fayer. *Voices of Freedom: An Oral History of the Civil Rights Movement from the 1950s through the 1980s.* New York: Bantam, 1991.

This penetrating study of the civil rights movement is the companion text to the acclaimed public television series *Eyes on the Prize,* which Fayer wrote and Hampton produced. The book is arranged chronologically and includes stirring personal reminiscences that tell of the courage and determination of those who risked their lives in the struggle for civil rights.

King, Martin Luther, Jr. *Why We Can't Wait.* New York: NAL-Dutton, Mentor, 1991.

King's 1963 "Letter from Birmingham Jail" is included in this handbook on nonviolent protest and civil disobedience, first published in 1964. King details the goals and strategies of the civil rights movement, focusing on why African Americans can no longer wait for others to address the problems of racism, poverty, and violence.

————. *The Trumpet of Conscience.* New York: Harper & Row, 1989.

This series of five radio broadcasts, prepared late in 1967 as part of the annual Massey Lectures, reflects King's philosophy in the final months before his death. Committed to fighting racism, poverty, and war anywhere in the world, King argues that mass civil disobedience is needed to force profound change and preserve human dignity.

Kluger, Richard. *Simple Justice: The History of* Brown v. Board of Education *and Black America's Struggle for Equality.* New York: Random House, Vintage, 1977.

The landmark case outlawing segregation in public schools is the centerpiece of this carefully researched, thought-provoking history of the legal struggle of African Americans for equal rights.

McAdam, Doug. *Freedom Summer.* New York: Oxford University Press, 1990.

During the summer of 1964, more than 1,000 college students traveled to the South to help register African-American voters. The experience changed their lives. This book tells their story.

Meier, August, and Elliott Rudwick. *CORE: A Study in the Civil Rights Movement, 1942–1968.* Champaign: University of Illinois Press, 1975.

The Congress of Racial Equality was founded in 1942 as a small, interracial group dedicated to nonviolent direct action. Twenty years later it had become a major force in the civil rights struggle. This valuable study reveals CORE's rise to prominence and its decline.

Meier, August, John H. Bracey, Jr., and Elliott Rudwick, eds. *Black Protest in the Sixties.* 2nd ed. New York: Markus Wiener, 1991.

Essays from *The New York Times Magazine* trace the course of black protest during the 1960s from the early calls for nonviolent action to the turmoil of the black power movement. The editors' highly acclaimed introduction summarizes the history of black protest in the 1960s.

Miller, Keith D. *Voice of Deliverance: The Language of Martin Luther King, Jr., and Its Sources.* New York: Free Press, 1991.

This work examines the effectiveness of King's speeches and essays in galvanizing support for the civil rights movement. The author focuses on the ways in which the oral traditions of the African-American church as well as the sermons of white Protestant ministers and others influenced King's writings.

Morris, Aldon D. *The Origins of the Civil Rights Movement: Black Communities Organizing for Change.* New York: Free Press, 1986.

Focusing on the early years of the civil rights movement, the author tells the story of the "ordinary" people who organized for action on the local level and eventually became the movement's foot soldiers.

Proudfoot, Merrill. *Diary of a Sit-in.* 2nd ed. Champaign: University of Illinois Press, 1990.

The author describes the experiences of the college students in Greensboro, North Carolina, who began a protest that helped spark the civil rights movement.

Robinson, Armstead L., and Patricia Sullivan, eds. *New Directions in Civil Rights Studies.* Charlottesville: University Press of Virginia, 1991.

This collection of essays, written by such civil rights activists and scholars as Julian Bond, Vincent Harding, James Farmer, Gavin Wright, and August Meier, offers a reassessment of the history of the civil rights movement and examines the questions that need to be researched in future studies.

Terry, Wallace. *Bloods: An Oral History of the Vietnam War by Black Veterans.* New York: Ballantine, 1985.

Powerful personal accounts describe the experiences of African-American soldiers who served their country in Vietnam against the backdrop of the civil rights struggle at home.

Tushnet, Mark V. *The NAACP's Legal Strategy against Segregated Education, 1925–1950.*   Chapel Hill: University of North Carolina Press, 1987.

In this insightful history the author describes how the NAACP collected funds, planned tactics, and mobilized the community to secure equal educational opportunities for all.

Weisbrot, Robert. *Freedom Bound: A History of America's Civil Rights Movement.*   New York: NAL-Dutton, Plume Books, 1991.

This history provides an excellent overview of the civil rights movement from 1955 to 1970. The work includes a rich collection of photographs.

Williams, Juan. *Eyes on the Prize: America's Civil Rights Years, 1954–1965.*   New York: Viking Penguin, 1988.

A companion volume to the prize-winning public television series of the same name, this insightful study recounts the history of the civil rights movement and tells how victory was achieved by nonviolent means in a violent society.

Zangrando, Robert L. *The NAACP Crusade against Lynching, 1909–1950.*   Philadelphia: Temple University Press, 1980.

The long and difficult campaign the NAACP waged against the murderous practice of lynching is the focus of this book.

Biographies and Autobiographies

Angelou, Maya. *I Know Why the Caged Bird Sings.*   New York: Bantam, 1983.

In this powerful autobiography Angelou describes her experiences growing up in the rural South during the 1930s.

Blackett, R.J.M., ed. *Thomas Morris Chester, Black Civil War Correspondent: His Dispatches from the Virginia Front.*   Baton Rouge: Louisiana State University Press, 1989.

The African-American educator, lawyer, and journalist who covered the Civil War as a correspondent for the *Philadelphia Press* is the subject of this fascinating biography.

Blight, David W. *Frederick Douglass' Civil War: Keeping Faith in Jubilee.* Baton Rouge: Louisiana State University Press, 1989.

This account of Douglass's life focuses on the abolitionist's experiences and activities during the Civil War. The author also raises new questions about the effects of that war on the lives of African Americans.

Carroll, John M. *Fritz Pollard: Pioneer in Racial Advancement.* Champaign: University of Illinois Press, 1991.

Frederick Douglass Pollard, an all-American football player at Brown University, became the first African-American head coach in the National Football League (NFL).

Cooper, Wayne F. *Claude McKay: Rebel Sojourner in the Harlem Renaissance.* Baton Rouge: Louisiana State University Press, 1987.

This portrait explores the work of one of the pioneers of African-American literature in the twentieth century.

Douglass, Frederick. *Narrative of the Life of Frederick Douglass, An American Slave.* Edited by Houston A. Baker, Jr. New York: Viking Penguin, 1982.

In 1845, just after Douglass gained his freedom, he wrote this moving account of his experiences under slavery.

Duberman, Martin B. *Paul Robeson.* New York: Ballantine, 1990.

The actor, singer, and political activist lived by uncompromising principles that led him to champion the causes of the disadvantaged without regard for his own career. This book focuses on the life of this complex man.

Franklin, John Hope, and August Meier, eds. *Black Leaders of the Twentieth Century.* Champaign: University of Illinois Press, 1982.

Booker T. Washington, W.E.B. Du Bois, Marcus Garvey, Mary McLeod Bethune, Mabel K. Staupers, Martin Luther King, Jr., and Malcolm X are among the 15 leaders profiled in this scholarly volume.

Garrow, David J.   *Bearing the Cross: Martin Luther King, Jr., and the Southern Christian Leadership Conference.*   New York: Random House, Vintage, 1987.

Based on hundreds of interviews and some of King's own papers, this thorough account traces the transformation of Martin Luther King, Jr., from a 26-year-old minister to an international symbol of nonviolence and civil rights.

Gates, Henry L., Jr., ed.   *Bearing Witness: Selections from African-American Autobiography in the Twentieth Century.*   New York: Pantheon Books, 1991.

These autobiographical sketches chronicle the lives and times of contemporary African Americans.

Goldman, Peter L.   *The Death and Life of Malcolm X.*   2nd ed. Champaign: University of Illinois Press, 1979.

The life story of Malcolm X offers insights into why, despite the lapse of years, this African-American freedom fighter is still a hero to people around the world.

Greene, Lorenzo J.   *Working with Carter G. Woodson, the Father of Black History: A Diary, 1928–1930.*   Baton Rouge: Louisiana State University Press, 1989.

Written by an associate of Woodson's and a prominent scholar in his own right, this personal account provides a firsthand look at Woodson's work as the founder of the Association for the Study of Negro Life and History, an organization dedicated to the study of African-American history.

Hamilton, Charles V.   *Adam Clayton Powell, Jr.: The Political Biography of an American Dilemma.*   New York: Macmillan, Atheneum, 1991.

The author chronicles the life of the powerful political and religious leader from Harlem.

Harlan, Louis.   *Booker T. Washington.*   2 vols. New York: Oxford University Press, 1972–1986.

These well-written, thoughtful volumes explore the life of the black leader and educator who founded the Tuskegee Institute.

Hurston, Zora Neale.   *Dust Tracks on the Road: An Autobiography.*
New York: HarperCollins, 1991.

Hurston's stirring autobiography traces her life from her
childhood in a Florida farm town to her success as a novelist,
folklorist, and anthropologist.

Kerman, Cynthia E., and Richard Eldridge.   *The Lives of Jean
Toomer: A Hunger for Wholeness.*   Baton Rouge: Louisiana State
University Press, 1989.

The writer and poet Jean Toomer, who emerged during the
Harlem Renaissance with her 1923 book entitled *Cane,* is the
focus of this biography.

Linnemann, Russell, ed.   *Alain Locke: Reflections on a Modern
Renaissance Man.*   Baton Rouge: Louisiana State University Press,
1982.

Locke was the first African American to be awarded a Rhodes
scholarship. As a professor at Howard University, he influenced
the lives of many young people. These biographical essays
describe various facets of Locke's life.

Litwack, Leon F., and August Meier, eds.   *Black Leaders of the
Nineteenth Century.*   Champaign: University of Illinois Press,
1991.

Sixteen essays analyzing the achievements of African-American
leaders of the 1800s offer new insights into the unique
personalities of those studied as well as interesting reflections on
the dynamics of black leadership of the time.

Loveland, Anne C.   *Lillian Smith: A Southerner Confronting the
South.*   Baton Rouge: Louisiana State University Press, 1986.

Lillian Smith was a writer, civil rights activist, and noteworthy
intellectual figure of the South. Her first novel, *Strange Fruit*
(1944), which describes the tragic ending of an interracial
romance, created a nationwide controversy.

Malcolm X.   *The Autobiography of Malcolm X.*   As told to Alex
Haley. New York: Ballantine, 1992.

This powerful, highly readable account, a collaboration with Alex
Haley, reveals the personal experiences of the complex,
charismatic civil rights leader.

Manning, Kenneth R. *Black Apollo of Science: The Life of Ernest Everett Just.* New York: Oxford University Press, 1983.

The pioneering American biologist and the first recipient of the Springarn Medal is the subject of this highly readable biography. Just began teaching at Howard University in 1907; for nearly 20 years he spent the summers conducting research at the laboratories at Woods Hole. He moved to Europe during the last years of his life, attempting to escape the racial discrimination hindering his work in the United States.

McFeely, William S. *Frederick Douglass.* New York: Norton, 1990.

In this penetrating biography the author offers an assessment of the complexity and vulnerability of the celebrated abolitionist.

Murray, Pauli. *Pauli Murray: The Autobiography of a Black Activist, Feminist, Lawyer, Priest, and Poet.* Knoxville: University of Tennessee Press, 1989.

Murray tells her own story in this autobiography of the magnificent rebel who made significant contributions to the civil rights and feminist movements.

Oates, Stephen B. *Let the Trumpet Sound: The Life of Martin Luther King, Jr.* New York: NAL-Dutton, Mentor, 1991.

This biography traces King's religious, intellectual, and political development. Incorporating interviews with those who knew King as well as previously unused materials from presidential libraries and from the Martin Luther King, Jr., Center in Atlanta, the work has been praised as one of the most comprehensive accounts of King's life.

Pfeffer, Paula F. *A. Philip Randolph: Pioneer of the Civil Rights Movement.* Baton Rouge: Louisiana State University Press, 1990.

The author chronicles the life of the famous labor leader, focusing on Randolph's role as a pioneer for civil rights.

Rampersad, Arnold. *The Life of Langston Hughes.* 2 vols. New York: Oxford University Press, 1986–1989.

The celebrated poet and writer is the subject of these highly readable, absorbing volumes. The work offers new insights into Hughes's personality and work as well as the times in which he lived.

Rose, Phyllis. *Jazz Cleopatra: Josephine Baker in Her Time.* New York: Random House, Vintage, 1990.

This biography tells the story of the legendary entertainer who became an international sensation.

Schwinger, Loren, ed. *The Autobiography of James Thomas.* Columbia: University of Missouri Press, 1984.

This poignant story traces the life of James Thomas, an African American who was born in 1827, went into business and became wealthy in St. Louis, and died there in poverty in 1913.

Simonsen, Thordis, ed. *You May Plow Here: The Narrative of Sara Brooks.* New York: Simon & Schuster, Touchstone Books, 1987.

Based on hundreds of hours of interviews, this portrait offers a vivid description of life in the rural South. The work has an added dimension in that Brooks includes in her story her migration to the North and her adjustment to urban living.

Suggs, Henry L. *P. B. Young, Newspaperman: Race, Politics, and Journalism in the New South, 1910–1962.* Charlottesville: University Press of Virginia, 1988.

The story of P. B. Young tells of a journalist and community leader who spent more than 50 years editing a Norfolk newspaper.

Tucker, Mark. *Ellington: The Early Years.* Champaign: University of Illinois Press, 1990.

The early years of this gifted musician's famous career are the focus of this biography, which traces Ellington's experiences from Washington, D.C., to Harlem.

Van Sertima, Ivan, ed. *Great Black Leaders, Ancient and Modern.* New Brunswick, N.J.: Transaction Publishers, 1988.

A variety of fascinating profiles describe the lives and times of outstanding African and African-American leaders.

Walker, Juliet E. *Free Frank: A Black Pioneer on the Antebellum Frontier.* Lexington: University Press of Kentucky, 1983.

This portrait tells the story of Frank McWhorter, an enslaved African American who eventually purchased his freedom, moved west, and founded a town in western Illinois. McWhorter is an ancestor of the author.

Washington, Booker T. *Up from Slavery.* New York: Carol Publishing, University Books, 1989.

Originally published in 1901, this autobiography chronicles Washington's personal journey from slavery to national prominence. Widely regarded as the most influential African American of his time, Washington was best known for his work as founder and head of the Tuskegee Institute.

Wells, Ida B. *Crusade for Justice: The Autobiography of Ida B. Wells.* Edited by Alfreda M. Duster. Chicago: University of Chicago Press, 1972.

The journalist and reformer known for her tireless campaign against lynching tells her own story in this personal account.

The Arts, Sports, and Entertainment

Andrews, William L. *To Tell a Free Story: The First Century of Afro-American Autobiography, 1760–1865.* Champaign: University of Illinois Press, 1986.

This examination of early African-American literature focuses on the theme of freedom. The author's thesis is that these early writings did more than talk about freedom as a goal; they actually became manifestations of that freedom.

Ashe, Arthur R. *A Hard Road to Glory: The History of the African-American Athlete.* 3 vols. New York: Warner Books, 1988.

These thoroughly researched and highly readable volumes chronicle the history of African-American athletes. Volume 1 covers the period from 1619 to 1918. Volume 2 covers the period from 1919 to 1945. Volume 3 covers the period from 1946 to the present.

Bell, Bernard W. *The Afro-American Novel and Its Tradition.* Amherst: University of Massachusetts Press, 1987.

The history of African-American fiction is the subject of this significant literary study, which highlights some 150 works and provides close readings of 41 novelists.

Bogle, Donald. *Blacks in American Films and Television: An Encyclopedia.* New York: Simon & Schuster, Fireside, 1989.

Names, credits, plot summaries, reviews—all are included in this useful reference that focuses on blacks in the American film and television industries.

Brown, Sterling A., Arthur P. Davis, and Ulysses Lee, eds. *The Negro Caravan.* Salem, N.H.: Ayer, 1969.

First published in 1941, this anthology of African-American literature includes poetry, short stories, excerpts from novels, folktales, drama, biography, and essays.

Dates, Jannette L., and William Barlow, eds. *Split Image: African Americans in the Mass Media.* Washington, D.C.: Howard University Press, 1990.

This collection of essays forms a comprehensive study of the changing image of African Americans in various mass media— music, films, radio, television, news, and advertising.

Davis, Arthur P., J. Saunders Redding, and Joyce Ann Joyce, eds. *The New Cavalcade: African-American Writing from 1760 to the Present.* 2 vols. Washington, D.C.: Howard University Press, 1991–1992.

Examining more than 300 selections that represent the work of more than 140 authors, these volumes trace the evolution of African-American writing and explore the historical contexts that shaped its development. Arranged chronologically, the selections include short stories and poems as well as excerpts from novels, essays, plays, biographies, and autobiographies.

Ely, Melvin P. *The Adventures of Amos 'n Andy: A Social History of an American Phenomenon.* New York: Free Press, 1991.

The author describes how a radio comedy show about two black men from the South became for many a symbol of the black experience.

Evans, Mari, ed. *Black Women Writers, 1950–1980: A Critical Evaluation.* New York: Doubleday, Anchor Press, 1984.

The personal reflections of 15 contemporary black women writers as well as critical evaluations of their work are contained in this insightful study. Included are such writers as Maya Angelou, Gwendolyn Brooks, Toni Morrison, and Alice Walker.

Fabre, Michel. *From Harlem to Paris: Black American Writers in France, 1840–1980.* Champaign: University of Illinois Press, 1991.

This work focuses on the lives of several talented African-American writers who moved to France to pursue their literary careers.

Goss, Linda, and Marian E. Barnes, eds. *Talk That Talk: An Anthology of African-American Storytelling.* New York: Simon & Schuster, Touchstone Books, 1989.

The rich, oral tradition of African-American storytelling is the centerpiece of this collection, which includes selections that range from animal legends and slave stories to comedy monologues and rap routines.

Hartigan, Lynda Roscoe. *Sharing Traditions: Five Black Artists in Nineteenth-Century America.* Washington, D.C.: Smithsonian Institution Press, 1985.

The African and American heritages reflected in the works of sculptor Edmonia Lewis and painters Joshua Johnson, Robert Scott Duncanson, Edward Mitchell Bannister, and Henry Ossawa Tanner are the subject of this richly illustrated volume.

Hedgepeth, Chester M., Jr. *Twentieth-Century African-American Writers and Artists.* Chicago: American Library Association, 1991.

Contemporary African-American artists from the fields of music, literature, painting, and sculpture are profiled in this valuable reference. The entry for each artist includes sections titled Biography, Criticism, Works by, and Works about.

Hoose, Phillip M. *Necessities: Racial Barriers in American Sports.* New York: Random House, 1989.

The author assesses the effects of racism in American sports.

Hughes, Langston, and Milton Meltzer. *Black Magic: A Pictorial History of the African American in the Performing Arts.* New York: Da Capo Press, 1990.

First published in 1967, this comprehensive work traces the achievements of African-American entertainers from the days of slavery to the late 1960s. Included are the fascinating stories of singers, dancers, musicians, composers, actors, and writers.

Kellner, Bruce, ed. *The Harlem Renaissance: An Historical Dictionary for the Era.* New York: Routledge, Chapman & Hall, 1987.

Alphabetical entries that include biographies of actors, musicians, and writers; book synopses; articles about key African-American leaders; references to plays and musical comedies; and descriptions of significant political and social developments are all included in this indispensable volume on the Harlem Renaissance.

Long, Richard A. *The Black Tradition in American Dance.* New York: Rizzoli International, 1989.

The author traces the development of African dance traditions as they evolved as a major form of artistic expression in the United States.

McElroy, Guy C., and Henry L. Gates, Jr. *Facing History: The Black Image in American Art, 1710–1940.* San Francisco: Bedford Arts, 1990.

Developed for the "Facing History" exhibit at the Corcoran Gallery, this richly illustrated book provides an important visual record of the African-American experience.

Page, James A. *Black Olympian Medalists.* Englewood, Colo.: Libraries Unlimited, 1991.

Along with biographies of individual black Olympic medalists, this carefully researched volume includes statistical data as well as a listing of international Olympians by sponsoring country.

Peterson, Robert. *Only the Ball Was White: A History of Legendary Black Players and All-Black Professional Teams.* New York: Oxford University Press, 1992.

When Peterson originally published this book in 1970, he revealed to many people for the first time the accomplishments of such baseball pioneers as Bud Fowler and Moses Fleetwood

Walker. In 1872 Fowler became the first African American to play with an integrated team. Walker became the first African-American major leaguer in 1884. The author also tells the story of the early Negro leagues in the days before the color barrier was broken in professional baseball.

Roberts, John W. *From Trickster to Badman: The Black Folk Hero in Slavery and Freedom.* Philadelphia: University of Pennsylvania Press, 1990.

The changing image of the black folk hero is the subject of this study.

Sanders, Leslie C. *The Development of Black Theater in America: From Shadows to Selves.* Baton Rouge: Louisiana State University Press, 1988.

The author traces the rich heritage of the African-American theater and examines the development of its unique traditions.

Southern, Eileen. *Biographical Dictionary of Afro-American and African Musicians.* Westport, Conn.: Greenwood Press, 1982.

This comprehensive volume chronicles the achievements of more than 1,500 African-American and African musicians who have played a significant role in the history of black music. The book describes the work of composers, performers, and educators in fields such as folk, popular, jazz, religious, and classical music.

Vercoutter, Jean, et al., eds. *The Image of the Black in Western Art.* 4 vols. Houston: The Menil Foundation, 1976–1989.

Handsomely illustrated and exhaustively researched, this series explores the portrayal of Africans and African Americans in Western art from ancient Egypt to World War I. The volumes offer new insights into the field of art history as well as the study of the black experience.

Wardlaw, Alvia J., et al. *Black Art: Ancestral Legacy: The African Impulse in African-American Art.* Edited by Robert V. Rozelle. Dallas: Dallas Museum of Art, 1989.

Exploring the influence of African art on artists in Europe and North America, this book gives special attention to the work of black artists in the Caribbean.

Willis-Thomas, Deborah. *Black Photographers, 1840–1940: An Illustrated Bio-Bibliography.* Hamden, Conn.: Garland, 1985.

The work of some 70 black photographers active during the first century of photography is presented in this valuable reference.

———. *Black Photographers, 1940–1988: An Illustrated Bio-Bibliography.* Hamden, Conn.: Garland, 1989.

Organized alphabetically, this volume presents biographical sketches and a selected bibliography for more than 400 black photographers of the last 50 years. Nearly half of the entries include a selection of photographs that illustrate the subject's work.

Woll, Allen. *Black Musical Theatre: From Coontown to Dreamgirls.* Baton Rouge: Louisiana State University Press, 1989.

This book traces the history of black musical theater from Reconstruction to the present. The study includes a fine collection of photographs.

Contemporary Issues

Asante, Molefi K. *The Afrocentric Idea.* Philadelphia: Temple University Press, 1988.

In this critique of the interpretation of African history and culture, the author defines the concept of Afrocentrism and explores ways in which the African heritage—as viewed from an African perspective—has shaped the past and continues to enrich the lives of African Americans.

Baldwin, James. *The Fire Next Time.* New York: Dell, Laurel Editions, 1985.

The celebrated writer, expressing the protest spirit of the sixties, vigorously attacks racism and its effects on both blacks and whites and explores the anger and frustration of searching for identity in American society.

Barker, Lucius J., and Ronald W. Walters, eds. *Jesse Jackson's 1984 Presidential Campaign: Challenge and Change in American Politics.* Champaign: University of Illinois Press, 1989.

Fourteen observers of the 1984 presidential election examine Jackson's candidacy and pose theoretical models for successful political campaigns by African Americans.

Bell, Derrick. *And We Are Not Saved: The Elusive Quest for Racial Justice.* New York: Basic Books, 1989.

In this creative study the author, a law professor, employs ten metaphorical tales to examine civil rights issues. The work addresses such subjects as slavery and the Constitution, affirmative action, black voting power, segregation, crime, and poverty.

Blauner, Bob. *Black Lives, White Lives: Three Decades of Race Relations in America.* Berkeley: University of California Press, 1989.

Blauner highlights changes in race relations in the United States over a 30-year period. The material is based on a series of interviews conducted in northern California with European Americans and African Americans regarding their racial consciousness and experiences.

Boyette, Michael, and Randi Boyette. *Let It Burn! The Philadelphia Tragedy.* Chicago: Contemporary Books, 1989.

This book focuses on the radical group MOVE and its tragic 1985 confrontation with the Philadelphia police department.

Carter, Stephen L. *Reflections of an Affirmative Action Baby.* New York: Basic Books, 1991.

This study of the issues surrounding affirmative action has something that many others do not have—the point of view of one who has been a beneficiary.

Cheatham, Harold E., and James B. Stewart, eds. *Black Families: Interdisciplinary Perspectives.* New Brunswick, N.J.: Transaction Publishers, 1990.

A series of articles explores the black family from a variety of approaches, including historical, societal, and economic.

Cross, William E., Jr. *Shades of Black: Diversity in African-American Identity.* Philadelphia: Temple University Press, 1991.

Written by a university psychologist, this book explores the stages of black identity development. The author finds that the themes of mental health, especially those of adaptive strength, are critical to the process. His work refutes earlier studies that suggested that conscious or unconscious self-hatred is a dominant theme of African-American identity.

Edsall, Thomas B., and Mary D. Edsall. *Chain Reaction: The Impact of Race, Rights, and Taxes on American Politics.* New York: Norton, 1991.

In this work the authors examine the factors that influence American politics, focusing especially on the impact of race.

Gaillard, Frye. *The Dream Long Deferred.* Chapel Hill: University of North Carolina Press, 1988.

Gaillard, editor of the *Charlotte Observer,* captures the human emotions and political implications involved in the issue of school busing in Charlotte, North Carolina, during the 1970s.

Goldfield, David R. *Black, White and Southern: Race Relations and Southern Culture, 1940 to the Present.* Baton Rouge: Louisiana State University Press, 1991.

This book examines the evolution of Southern race relations over the past 50 years, focusing especially on the effects of the civil rights movement on the South's unique culture.

Jackson, Jesse L. *Straight from the Heart.* Edited by Roger D. Hatch and Frank E. Watkins. Rev. ed. Minneapolis: Augsburg Fortress, 1987.

Jackson's fervor and zeal for his vision of a just society are captured in this collection of 36 of his speeches, sermons, eulogies, essays, and interviews.

Jaynes, Gerald D., and Robin M. Williams, Jr., eds. *A Common Destiny: Blacks and American Society.* Washington, D.C.: National Academy Press, 1990.

The National Research Council commissioned this major research effort. The findings of the scholars contributing to the study are both informative and provocative.

Jencks, Christopher, and Paul E. Peterson, eds. *The Urban Underclass.* Washington, D.C.: Brookings Institution, 1991.

A series of essays focuses on the people who are a part of what is defined as the underclass of today's American cities.

Kaufman, Jonathan. *Broken Alliance: The Turbulent Times between Blacks and Jews in America.* New York: NAL-Dutton, 1989.

By telling the personal stories of six people, this controversial book traces the changing relationship between Jews and African Americans in the United States over the past 20 years.

Kozol, Jonathan. *Savage Inequalities: Children in America's Schools.* New York: Crown, 1991.

This powerful and disturbing study reveals the vast differences in the quality of public education between urban and suburban schools—schools that to a large degree remain racially segregated.

Leigh, Wilhelmina, and James B. Stewart, eds. *The Housing Status of Black Americans.* New Brunswick, N.J.: Transaction Publishers, 1992.

The status of housing for African Americans in the post-civil-rights era is the subject of this series of essays.

Marable, Manning. *Black American Politics: From the Washington Marches to Jesse Jackson.* Rev. ed. New York: Routledge, Chapman & Hall, 1991.

Beginning with a synthesis of political movements in Africa, the Caribbean, and the United States, this scholarly work emphasizes the link between the history of African-American politics and the history of class struggle.

Orfield, Gary, and Carole Ashkinaze. *The Closing Door: Conservative Policy and Black Opportunity.* Chicago: University of Chicago Press, 1991.

This book is the first to result from the Metropolitan Opportunity Project, a five-year study documenting the impact of recent conservative policies on the nation's minority groups. Focusing on the city of Atlanta, the authors use both statistical data and personal stories to present a disturbing view of the decline in opportunities for African Americans in urban America.

Powell-Hopson, Darlene, and Derek S. Hopson. *Different and Wonderful: Raising Black Children in a Race-Conscious Society.* Englewood Cliffs, N.J.: Prentice-Hall, 1990.

Written by two clinical psychologists, this insightful guide to child development offers a wide variety of practical ideas for helping African-American children become positive, self-respecting individuals. Especially useful is the section highlighting books, magazines, games, toys, and other resources that celebrate African-American culture.

Wilson, William Julius. *The Truly Disadvantaged: The Inner City, the Underclass, and Public Policy.* Chicago: University of Chicago Press, 1990.

The author provides a thought-provoking analysis of urban poverty, arguing that contemporary poverty is more a factor of economic changes than of racism and suggesting policies such as massive job-training programs and child-care services that could bring relief to the underclass.

Zweigenhaft, Richard L., and William G. Domhoff. *Blacks in the White Establishment? A Study of Race and Class in America.* New Haven: Yale University Press, 1991.

In 1963 a group of educators founded a program called A Better Chance (ABC), in which talented but disadvantaged African-American students were given the opportunity to attend elite prep schools. This book, based on interviews with 38 ABC graduates, examines the success of the program. ABC made it possible for students to overcome class barriers; most earned degrees from prestigious universities and moved into high-status professions. Yet many were unable to overcome racial barriers, ultimately being denied top positions because of color prejudice.

Resources for Multicultural Education

Theory

Baker, Gwendolyn. *Planning and Organizing for Multicultural Instruction.* Reading, Mass.: Addison-Wesley, 1983.

This work presents a foundation for multicultural education, proposes guidelines for implementing a multicultural curriculum, and offers specific strategies and sample lesson plans for multicultural education in a variety of disciplines and at different grade levels.

Banks, James A. *Multiethnic Education: Theory and Practice.* 2nd ed. Boston: Allyn & Bacon, 1988.

The author provides a thorough discussion of multiethnic education in this scholarly work, which is especially useful to readers with a fundamental understanding of the field.

————. *Teaching Strategies for Ethnic Studies.* 5th ed. Boston: Allyn & Bacon, 1991.

This book, which focuses on classroom instruction, includes a design to help teachers prepare material on comparative cultural studies and integrate multicultural content into their curriculum. The work also provides background information about the history of several different racial and ethnic groups in the United States.

Banks, James A., and Cherry A. McGee Banks, eds. *Multicultural Education: Issues and Perspectives.* Boston: Allyn & Bacon, 1989.

This collection of essays about multicultural education will assist teachers in working with students from various ethnic, cultural, religious, language, and social-class groups; students of both genders; and exceptional students.

Banks, James A., and James Lynch, eds. *Multicultural Education in Western Societies.* New York: Praeger, 1986.

The essays in this volume explore the development of multicultural education in several Western countries. In the final chapter the authors summarize their findings with recommendations for changes in today's educational programs.

Baptiste, H. Prentice, Jr., ed. *Multicultural Education: A Synopsis.* Lanham, Md.: University Press of America, 1979.

An excellent introduction to both multicultural and bilingual education is presented in this collection of essays. The work includes a review of selected multicultural publications and an assessment of teacher training models related to the field.

Baruth, Leroy G., and M. Lee Manning. *Multicultural Education of Children and Adolescents.* Boston: Allyn & Bacon, 1992.

The authors explore the concept of multicultural education and discuss how educators can address questions concerning cultural diversity and multiple perspectives. The four main sections of the text are Understanding Culture and Ethnicity in a Pluralistic Nation, Understanding Culturally Diverse Learners, Understanding Multicultural Education: Curriculum and Teaching Concerns, and Understanding the Future of Multicultural Education.

Bennett, Christine I. *Comprehensive Multicultural Education: Theory and Practice.* 2nd ed. Boston: Allyn & Bacon, 1990.

This book offers a practical approach to multicultural education, exploring both theory and practice. The text highlights the challenges today's teachers face in a multiethnic, multilingual, and multicultural school environment.

Boyer, James. *Multicultural Education: Product and Process.* Manhattan: Kansas Urban Education Center, 1985.

Included in this work are practical suggestions that curriculum committees and individual teachers will find useful as they attempt to add a multicultural dimension to their instructional programs.

Clark, Reginald M. *Family Life and School Achievement: Why Poor Black Children Succeed or Fail.* Chicago: University of Chicago Press, 1984.

Using case studies of African-American inner-city families, the author compares the processes that occur in families that produce high-achieving students with those that occur in families that produce low-achieving students. Arguing that success in school cannot be predicted based on social class or racial background, the author describes what families can do to help promote high achievement.

Garcia, Ricardo L. *Teaching in a Pluralistic Society: Concepts, Models, Strategies.* 2nd ed. New York: HarperCollins, 1991.

This introductory textbook explores the effects of ethnicity on learning and provides two models for pluralistic teaching. Role-playing and critical-thinking exercises are included.

Gollnick, Donna M., and Philip C. Chinn. *Multicultural Education in a Pluralistic Society.* 3rd ed. Columbus, Ohio: Macmillan, Merrill, 1990.

The diverse subcultures of American society, including those formed by language differences, are the subject of this study. The detailed descriptions can help educators identify the needs and special interests of their students.

Grant, Carl A., and Christine E. Sleeter. *After the School Bell Rings.* Philadelphia: Taylor & Francis, Falmer Press, 1986.

This case study investigates social relationships and equality in a Midwestern multiracial junior-high school by examining student and teacher behavior and cultural knowledge.

Hale-Benson, Janice E. *Black Children: Their Roots, Culture, and Learning Styles.* Rev. ed. Baltimore: Johns Hopkins University Press, 1986.

The author takes a multidisciplinary approach to explore the effects of African-American culture on childhood development and to suggest needed educational reforms.

Hernandez, Hilda. *Multicultural Education: A Teacher's Guide to Content and Process.* Columbus, Ohio: Macmillan, Merrill, 1989.

Drawing on research and practical examples, the author discusses the implications of multicultural education for classroom instruction, bilingualism, special education, curriculum development, and community-school relations.

National Association of State Boards of Education. *The American Tapestry: Educating a Nation.* Alexandria, Va.: National Association of State Boards of Education, 1991.

This guide to infusing multiculturalism in American education offers a series of recommendations to help students learn to respect the richness of the country's varied cultures and to help teachers understand the home environments and cultural experiences that shape how children learn.

National Council for the Social Studies. *Curriculum Guidelines for Multicultural Education: Position Statement.* Rev. ed. Washington, D.C.: National Council for the Social Studies, 1992.

A rationale for multicultural education, a series of curriculum guidelines, and a program evaluation checklist are included in this practical guide for educators.

Nieto, Sonia. *Affirming Diversity: The Sociopolitical Context of Multicultural Education.* White Plains, N.Y.: Longman, 1992.

Using a case study approach, the author discusses the meaning of multicultural education, explores its benefits for all students, and offers suggestions for classroom implementation.

Phinney, Jean S., and Mary J. Rotheram. *Children's Ethnic Socialization.* Beverly Hills: Sage Publications, 1986.

The impact of ethnic group differences on childhood development is the subject of this book, which concludes with a section on the themes of ethnic study and their implications.

Richard-Amato, Patricia A., and Marguerite Ann Snow, eds. *The Multicultural Classroom: Readings for Content-Area Teachers.* White Plains, N.Y.: Longman, 1992.

This collection of essays discusses how to adapt content areas such as social studies, literature, science, and mathematics to minority and language-minority students.

Shade, Barbara J. *Engaging the Battle for African-American Minds.* Washington, D.C.: National Alliance of Black School Educators, 1990.

This monograph focuses on the difficulties teachers may have in correctly interpreting the classroom behavior of African-American students. The author discusses how teachers can misread students and provides suggestions to help teachers recognize student qualities in terms of strengths rather than weaknesses.

_____, ed. *Culture, Style, and the Educative Process.* Springfield, Ill.: Charles C. Thomas, 1989.

Issues related to culture and cognitive style are addressed in this collection, which focuses on African Americans, Native Americans, and Mexican Americans. The first chapters review the literature on the subject; subsequent chapters consider the implications of the research for classroom teaching.

Sleeter, Christine E., ed. *Empowerment through Multicultural Education.* Albany: SUNY Press, 1991.

This series of essays can help preparing and practicing teachers understand how children who are members of oppressed groups view their world and what kinds of changes would promote their academic success and sense of power.

Sleeter, Christine E., and Carl A. Grant. *Making Choices for Multicultural Education: Five Approaches to Race, Class, and Gender.* Columbus, Ohio: Macmillan, Merrill, 1988.

Social studies educators will find this book very helpful as they make decisions in regard to multicultural education. Following a thorough review of articles and books on the subject, the authors present five approaches to multicultural education, each supported by research and methods for practical application.

Taylor, Denny, and Catherine Dorsey-Gaines. *Growing Up Literate: Learning from Inner-City Families.* Portsmouth, N.H.: Heinemann, 1988.

Based on in-depth studies of African-American families living in inner cities, the authors offer insights into the contexts within which children acquire literacy.

Thernstrom, Stephen, Ann Orlov, and Sean Handlin. *Harvard Encyclopedia of American Ethnic Groups.* Cambridge, Mass.: Harvard University Press, 1980.

A comprehensive reference for teachers and other professionals, this volume provides a systematic guide to the history, culture, and characteristics of more than 100 ethnic groups in the United States.

Practice

Anti-Defamation League of B'nai B'rith.   *The Wonderful World of Difference.*   New York: Anti-Defamation League of B'nai B'rith, 1992.

Twenty lessons for grades K to 8 provide educators with a starting point for helping students explore the richness of cultural diversity.

Aten, Jerry.   *Americans, Too!*   Carthage, Ill.: Good Apple, 1982.

Lesson plans for teaching about African Americans, Hispanic Americans, Asian Americans, and American Indians at grades 4 through 10 are included in this useful volume. The plans provide an overview of the history of each group and include a variety of research and discussion activities for students.

Baptiste, H. Prentice, Jr., and Mira L. Baptiste.   *Developing the Multicultural Process in Classroom Instruction: Competencies for Teachers.*   Lanham, Md.: University Press of America, 1979.

This volume presents a series of competencies related to multicultural education that were written and field tested by the authors.

Broderick, Dorothy M.   *The Image of the Black in Children's Fiction.* New York: Bowker, 1973.

The portrayal of African Americans in children's books published between 1827 and 1967 is the subject of this study, which reveals stereotypes and explores the social attitudes reflected during various time periods. The author's findings provide a useful historical background for those evaluating children's literature today.

Brown, Thomas J.   *Teaching Minorities More Effectively: A Model for Educators.*   Lanham, Md.: University Press of America, 1987.

This short, straightforward book offers a discussion of practical teaching strategies that productively engage inner-city students. Included are such topics as connecting material with student interests, increasing motivation, and preparing for assessment.

Cooperative Children's Book Center. *Multicultural Literature for Children and Young Adults.* 3rd ed. Edited by Ginny Moore Kruse and Kathleen T. Horning. Madison: University of Wisconsin Press and the Wisconsin Department of Public Instruction, 1991.

This annotated bibliography highlights children's literature by and about African Americans, American Indians, Asian Americans, and Hispanic Americans.

————. *The Multicolored Mirror: Cultural Substance in Literature for Children and Young Adults.* Edited by Merri V. Lindgren. Fort Atkinson, Wis.: Highsmith Press, 1991.

An overview of issues related to multicultural children's literature and a guide to resources are included in this useful volume. Part I contains articles written by educators, authors, illustrators, and publishers on such topics as Approaches to Authenticity in Illustration and Writing and Evaluating Books by and about African Americans. Part II contains resource listings of multicultural books for children and young adults.

Derman-Sparks, Louise, and the A.B.C. Task Force Staff. *Anti-Bias Curriculum: Tools for Empowering Young Children.* Washington, D.C.: National Association for the Education of Young Children, 1989.

The authors provide guidelines and suggest classroom activities to help preschoolers and kindergartners develop an appreciation for racial, cultural, gender, and physical differences.

Froschl, Merle, and Barbara Sprung, eds. *Resources for Educational Equity: An Annotated Bibliography and Guide for Grades Pre-Kindergarten–12.* New York: Garland, 1988.

This comprehensive compilation of resources that promote a bias-free classroom focuses mainly on sex equity but also includes references to materials addressing bias due to race and disability.

Grant, Carl A., and Christine E. Sleeter. *Turning on Learning.* Columbus, Ohio: Macmillan, Merrill, 1989.

A companion volume to *Making Choices for Multicultural Education* by Sleeter and Grant, this work provides lesson plans that illustrate how five different approaches to multicultural education can be used in various subject areas in grades 1 through 12.

Johnson, Dianne. *Telling Tales: The Pedagogy and Promise of African American Literature for Youth.* Westport, Conn.: Greenwood Press, 1990.

The development of children's literature written by African Americans to both educate and inspire young people is the subject of this study, which examines W.E.B. Du Bois's *The Brownies' Book* magazine, the works of Langston Hughes and Arna Bontemps, and the picture books of Lucille Clifton. The work also includes a valuable introduction to the field of African-American literature.

Kendall, Frances E. *Diversity in the Classroom: A Multicultural Approach to the Education of Young Children.* New York: Teachers College Press, 1983.

This teacher's resource offers both background information and practical suggestions for developing a multicultural classroom environment for young children.

King, Edith W. *Teaching Ethnic and Gender Awareness: Methods and Materials for the Elementary School.* 2nd ed. Dubuque, Iowa: Kendall-Hunt, 1989.

Developed for elementary teachers, particularly primary teachers, this resource includes discussions and lesson plans regarding how to promote children's understanding of ethnicity and gender in the classroom.

MacCann, Donnarae, and Gloria Woodard, eds. *The Black American in Books for Children: Readings in Racism.* 2nd ed. Metuchen, N.J.: Scarecrow Press, 1985.

The contributors to this collection of essays, first published in 1972, document examples of racism in children's books and encourage authors to write from a black perspective. Included are such articles as Nancy Larrick's "The All-White World of Children's Books" and Augusta Baker's "Guidelines for Black Books: An Open Letter to Juvenile Editors." Among other contributors are Julius Lester, Dorothy Sterling, and Joseph Okpaku.

————, eds. *Cultural Conformity in Books for Children: Further Readings in Racism.* Metuchen, N.J.: Scarecrow Press, 1977.

The editors of *The Black American in Books for Children* continue their work in this series of essays that examines Hispanic, Asian-American, African-American, and Native-American perspectives on such topics as racism in children's literature, book selection criteria, and methods of handling racist materials.

Martin Luther King, Jr., Center for Nonviolent Social Change. *Infusion Model for Teaching Dr. Martin Luther King, Jr.'s Nonviolent Principles in Schools.* Atlanta: Martin Luther King, Jr., Center for Nonviolent Social Change, 1989.

This valuable resource provides lesson plans for grades K through 12 that focus on King's life and family, the civil rights movement, and the principles of nonviolent change.

New York Public Library. *The Black Experience in Children's Books.* New York: New York Public Library, 1989.

Brief synopses of children's books by and about African Americans are presented in this annotated bibliography.

Portland Public Schools. *African-American Baseline Essays.* Rev. ed. Portland, Oreg.: Portland Public Schools, 1992.

This series of essays provides teachers with background information about the history, culture, and contributions of Africans and African Americans in various disciplines, including art, language arts, mathematics, science, social studies, and music.

Ramsey, Patricia G. *Teaching and Learning in a Diverse World: Multicultural Education for Young Children.* New York: Teachers College Press, 1986.

Useful for those teaching preschool to grade 3, this book offers creative ideas that serve as guidelines for a multicultural curriculum. The work cites research studies that provide a clear discussion of cultural awareness, including the controversies of bilingual education.

————. *Multicultural Education: A Source Book.* New York: Garland, 1989.

This book explores how early childhood education can help minimize prejudice.

Rollock, Barbara. *Black Authors and Illustrators of Children's Books: A Biographical Dictionary.* 2nd ed. New York: Garland, 1992.

Parents and teachers interested in identifying African-American authors and illustrators of children's books will find this volume indispensable. The entries are arranged alphabetically, and each includes a biographical sketch and a bibliography of the person's works.

Schniedewind, Nancy, and Ellen Davidson. *Open Minds to Equality: A Sourcebook of Learning Activities to Promote Race, Sex, Class, and Age Equity.* Englewood Cliffs, N.J.: Prentice-Hall, 1983.

This excellent sourcebook includes a structured progression of lesson plans to help students learn to work together cooperatively, reflect on the diversity of American culture, and develop skills to promote social justice in their environment.

Tiedt, Pamela L., and Iris M. Tiedt. *Multicultural Teaching: A Handbook of Activities, Information, and Resources.* 3rd ed. Boston: Allyn & Bacon, 1990.

A variety of creative ideas for integrating multicultural concepts in the classroom are offered in this activity-based text. The book explores the development of multicultural education in the United States, establishes objectives for multicultural education, and offers ideas for programs in different subject areas as well as for different age groups.

Additional References

For more information, you may wish to contact the following organizations:

American Federation of Teachers
Human Rights and Community Relations
Department
555 New Jersey Avenue, NW
Washington, DC 20001
(Written requests only)

Anti-Defamation League of B'nai B'rith
Contact your regional ADL office or:
A World of Difference Institute
823 United Nations Plaza
New York, NY 10017
(Written requests only)

Association for Supervision and Curriculum Development
Helené Hodges
Director of Research and Information
1250 North Pitt Street
Alexandria, VA 22314
(703) 549-9110, extension 515

Council on Interracial Books for Children
1841 Broadway, Room 608
New York, NY 10023
(212) 757-5339

The Journal of Negro Education
Howard University–West Campus
2900 Van Ness Street, NW
Washington, DC 20008
(Written requests only)

Multicultural Leader
Educational Materials and Service Center
P.O. Box 802
Edmonds, WA 98020
(Written requests only)

MultiCultural Review
Greenwood Publishing Group, Inc.
88 Post Road West, Box 5007
Westport, CT 06881
(203) 226-3571

National Alliance of Black School Educators
2816 Georgia Avenue, NW
Washington, DC 20001
(202) 483-1549

National Association for the Education of Young Children
1834 Connecticut Avenue, NW
Washington, DC 20009
(Written requests only)

National Association for Multicultural Education
c/o Dr. Rose M. Duhon-Sells, Chair
NAME Steering Committee
1703 Longview Drive
Baton Rouge, LA 70806
(504) 771-2290

National Association of State Boards of Education
   Publications Department
   1012 Cameron Street
   Alexandria, VA 22314
   (703) 684-4000

National Council for the Social Studies
   Information Services
   3501 Newark Street, NW
   Washington, DC 20016
   (Written requests only)

Teaching Tolerance
   400 Washington Avenue
   Montgomery, AL 36104
   (Written requests only)

Award-Winning and Notable Books for Children

Growing Up

Adoff, Arnold. *OUTside INside Poems.* Illustrated by John Steptoe. New York: Lothrop, Lee & Shepard, 1981. 32 pages.

The free-verse poems in this book can be read individually or as a continuing poetic narrative that explores the inner and outer life of an African-American boy who longs to be a baseball star. By emphasizing perspective, the book's illustrations convey both internal and external realities. (Ages 7–13)

———. *All the Colors of the Race.* Illustrated by John Steptoe. New York: Lothrop, Lee & Shepard, 1982. 64 pages.

Written from the point of view of a biracial child, this collection of free verse is a celebration of heritage, identity, and individuality. The poems, which can be read separately or as a continuous narrative, are accompanied by striking illustrations. (Ages 6–14)

———, ed. *My Black Me: A Beginning Book of Black Poetry.* New York: E.P. Dutton, 1974. 96 pages.

This collection of poems for young readers celebrates the African-American heritage, focusing on contemporary black leaders as well as those from the past. (Ages 8 and older)

Ahlberg, Allan. *. . . Starting School.* Illustrated by Janet Ahlberg. New York: Puffin, 1990. 32 pages.

This picture book follows eight children from their first and second days at school to the end of one week, several weeks, and several months. The children represent many racial and ethnic backgrounds. (Ages 2–6)

Bailey, Pearl. *Duey's Tale.* New York: Harcourt Brace Jovanovich, 1975. 59 pages.

This allegory, in which the main characters are a seed, a log, and a bottle, speaks of family, friendship, and growing up. (Ages 10 and older)

Blume, Judy. *Iggie's House.* New York: Dell, 1986. 128 pages.

This moving story deals with the integration of a black family into an all-white neighborhood. (Ages 8–11)

Bogart, Jo Ellen. *Daniel's Dog.* Illustrated by Janet Wilson. New York: Scholastic, 1992. 32 pages.

Young Daniel must adjust to the birth of a baby sister and the death of his grandfather. He copes by inventing an imaginary dog that he eventually shares with his playmate Norman. The bold illustrations skillfully depict the emotions of preschoolers. (Ages 3–6)

Boyd, Candy Dawson. *Circle of Gold.* New York: Scholastic, 1984. 128 pages.

Mattie enters a writing contest in hopes of earning money to buy a gift for her mother, who holds two jobs. At the same time Mattie must face the false accusations of a classmate. This fast-paced novel is set amidst the hustle and bustle of Chicago's South Side. (Ages 8–12)

————. *Breadsticks and Blessing Places.* New York: Macmillan, 1985. 216 pages.

An upbeat tone marks this real-life family story about a sixth-grader named Toni, who is hoping to qualify for admission to a better public school. At the same time she must come to grips with the accidental death of a friend. Among its other themes, this powerful novel explores the links between self-esteem and achievement. (Ages 10 and older)

————. *Charlie Pippin.* New York: Puffin, 1988. 192 pages.

A spirited young girl named Charlie hopes to understand her rigid father, a Vietnam veteran, by finding out everything she can about the Vietnam War. The themes of war, respect for authority, African-American roles, and relationships between family members are highlighted in this novel about confronting unresolved conflicts of the past. (Ages 11–14)

Brooks, Gwendolyn. *Bronzeville Boys and Girls.* Illustrated by Ronni Solbert. New York: Harper & Row, 1967. 48 pages.

This collection of poems by the celebrated poet and author reflects the everyday thoughts and emotions of young children learning about themselves and about the world around them. Engaging line drawings illustrate the poems. (Ages 8–11)

Caines, Jeannette. *Just Us Women.* Illustrated by Pat Cummings. New York: Harper & Row, 1984. 32 pages.

A young girl and her favorite aunt enjoy a car trip together to North Carolina. They stop along the way to explore whatever interests them, following no schedule other than their own. Their joy of being together is conveyed through the bold colors and unusual perspectives of the drawings. (Ages 4–7)

————. *I Need a Lunch Box.* Illustrated by Pat Cummings. New York: Harper & Row, 1988. 32 pages.

A boy watches his sister receive a new lunch box and wishes he had one for himself. The art and text transform an ordinary experience of sibling rivalry into a loving family portrait. (Ages 3–6)

Carlstrom, Nancy W. *Wild Wild Sunflower Child Anna.* Illustrated by Jerry Pinkney. New York: Macmillan, Aladdin, 1991. 32 pages.

Anna is an exuberant child with a sunny disposition and active imagination. This colorful picture book describes Anna's solitary escapade within a large backyard and nearby field and woods. Bright yellow-and-green watercolor washes complement the line drawings that illustrate the story. (Ages 3–6)

Childress, Alice. *A Hero Ain't Nothing But a Sandwich.* New York: Avon, Flare, 1977. 128 pages.

This dramatic and sensitive novel tells the story of Benjie, a boy on the verge of becoming a heroin addict. (Ages 13 and older)

————. *Rainbow Jordan.* New York: Avon, Flare, 1982. 128 pages.

Fourteen-year-old Rainbow tries hard to be strong and independent in a world of disappointment and uncertainty. Her mother has abandoned her once again in their New York City apartment, and she has been taken in by a woman who sets very high standards. Despite the pressures of coping with a delinquent mother, a foster parent, a friend involved in shoplifting, and a demanding boyfriend, Rainbow learns to be true to herself. (Ages 13 and older)

Clifton, Lucille. *Everett Anderson's Friend.* Illustrated by Ann Grifalconi. New York: Holt, Rinehart and Winston, 1976. 28 pages.

When Everett's new neighbor turns out to be a girl, he learns that girls can run and win at ball, too. This humorous tale shows how disappointment can be changed to delight. (Ages 5–7)

————. *Everett Anderson's Nine Month Long.* Illustrated by Ann Grifalconi. New York: Henry Holt, 1978. 32 pages.

Waiting for something special can be hard, as Everett learns as he prepares to welcome a new baby into the family. (Ages 5–7)

————. *My Friend Jacob.* Illustrated by Thomas DiGrazia. New York: E.P. Dutton, 1980. 32 pages.

This novel explores the friendship of a young boy named Sam and his neighbor Jacob, an adult who is developmentally impaired. The two learn many things from each other. Pencil drawings illustrate the poignant narrative. (Ages 3–8)

————. *The Boy Who Didn't Believe in Spring.* Illustrated by Brinton Turkle. New York: E.P. Dutton, 1988. 32 pages.

Tony and his friend King Shabaz search their city neighborhood to see if spring really exists. They finally find the first signs in a vacant lot with a nest of blue eggs and some little yellow flowers. (Ages 3–8)

————. *Everett Anderson's Goodbye.* Illustrated by Ann Grifalconi. New York: Henry Holt, 1988. 32 pages.

Elizabeth Kübler-Ross's five stages of grief are set within poetry to tell the story of the death of a father. Dramatic pencil drawings complement the emotional power of the short text. (Ages 3–8)

Curtis, Gavin. *Grandma's Baseball.* New York: Crown, 1990. 32 pages.

Changes in a boy's household take place when Grandma moves in to live with his family. There is oatmeal for breakfast, little after-school leisure, and, above all, no slamming of the screen door. The boy's relationship with Grandma improves with the appearance of an autographed baseball from Grandpa's days as a player on the Kansas City Monarchs. (Ages 4–7)

De Veaux, Alexis. *An Enchanted Hair Tale.* Illustrated by Cheryl Hanna. New York: HarperCollins, 1991. 48 pages.

Sudan's long braids set him apart from other children, who tease him because he is different. When Sudan meets a whole family with enchanted hair, he learns to celebrate his differences and to think more positively about himself. Rhyming text and engaging black-and-white pencil drawings make this a captivating story. (Ages 5–8)

Dragonwagon, Crescent. *Half a Moon and One Whole Star.* Illustrated by Jerry Pinkney. New York: Macmillan, Aladdin, 1990. 32 pages.

As young Susan sleeps snug in her bed, rhyming verses describe the nighttime world in her yard and neighborhood. Beautiful, watercolor paintings reinforce the themes of love and security. (Ages 3–8)

———. *Home Place.* Illustrated by Jerry Pinkney. New York: Macmillan, 1990. 40 pages.

A man, a woman, and a school-aged girl are hiking in a daffodil field when they discover a nail, a small yellow bottle, a china doll's arm, and other artifacts. The hikers realize that a house must have stood on the spot at one time. Beautiful, full-color illustrations invite readers to join the hikers in imagining the activities and conversations of an African-American family living in the house in days gone by. (Ages 7–10)

Fields, Julia. *The Green Lion of Zion Street.* Illustrated by Jerry Pinkney. New York: Macmillan, McElderry, 1988. 32 pages.

Bored while waiting for a bus on a wintry day, a group of children imagine that a lion statue has come to life. Written in black English, Fields's free-form poem is full of creative, childlike imagery. Pencil-and-watercolor paintings capture the spirit of the children at play. (Ages 4–9)

Florian, Douglas. *City Street.* New York: Greenwillow, 1990. 32 pages.

Simple, rhyming phrases provide the complete text for each two-page picture spread depicting city life. The full-color visual images present the diversity of people in city neighborhoods and show their varied activities. (Ages 2–5)

Flournoy, Valerie. *The Patchwork Quilt.* Illustrated by Jerry Pinkney. New York: Dial Books, 1985. 32 pages.

Grandma has been making a patchwork memory quilt using colorful fabric from all of the members of her family. When Grandma cannot work on the quilt any longer, Tanya decides to continue the beautiful family record. Tanya even finds a new way to link the present and the past. (Ages 5–9)

Giovanni, Nikki. *Ego-tripping and Other Poems for Young People.* Illustrated by George Ford. New York: Lawrence Hill Books, 1974. 37 pages.

This powerful collection of poems explores love, loneliness, and the dreams of youth as well as the strength and pride of the African-American heritage. (Ages 8–13)

————. *Spin a Soft Black Song: Poems for Children.* Rev. ed. Illustrated by George Martins. New York: Farrar, Straus & Giroux, 1987. 64 pages.

The author's volunteer activities for the Reading Is Fundamental program led to the writing of these 35 poems. Illustrated with black-and-white drawings, the poems observe, celebrate, and lament the children's lives. (Ages 7–14)

Greenfield, Eloise. *Darlene.* Illustrated by George Ford. New York: Routledge, Chapman & Hall; Methuen, 1980. 32 pages.

Darlene, who uses a wheelchair, waits for her mother to pick her up from a cousin's home. All children can relate to Darlene's impatience and determination. (Ages 3–6)

————. *Daydreamers.* Illustrated by Tom Feelings. New York: Dial Books, 1985. 32 pages.

This collection of short poems portrays children in introspective poses. The poems reflect the hopes and fears of childhood. (Ages 9–14)

————. *Honey, I Love, and Other Love Poems.* Illustrated by Diane and Leo Dillon. New York: Harper & Row, Trophy, 1986. 48 pages.

The 16 poems in this collection focus on the experiences a young African-American girl, expressing her childlike observations and appreciation for everyday life. (Ages 6–9)

————. *Sister.* Illustrated by Moneta Barnett. New York: Harper & Row, Trophy, 1987. 96 pages.

As 13-year-old Doretha reads through her diary, remembering both good times and bad times from the last four years, she learns more about herself and her family. (Ages 10–12)

————. *Nathaniel Talking.* Illustrated by Jan Spivey Gilchrist. New York: Writers & Readers, 1988. 32 pages.

This handsome collection of 18 first-person poems characterizes the strong moods and lively experiences of a nine-year-old boy named Nathaniel. The poems also introduce readers to "bones," the instrument played by Nathaniel's grandma and by elders in Africa as well as in the United States. By looking at the past, present, and future through a child's eyes, these poems create a sense of hope and pride. (Ages 5–11)

————. *First Pink Light.* Illustrated by Jan Spivey Gilchrist. New York: Writers & Readers, 1991. 32 pages.

In this loving family portrait, a young boy named Tyree convinces his mother to let him stay up for his father's return. The story focuses on the various emotions Tyree experiences during the wait—his elation with the cardboard fort he hides in while his mother does her homework, his transparent efforts to get his way, and his welcome surrender to sleep. (Ages 4–9)

————. *Grandpa's Face.* Illustrated by Floyd Cooper. New York: Putnam, Philomel, 1991. 32 pages.

Tamika's grandfather is a professional actor with an expressive face. One day Tamika is sure that her grandfather's stern look is directed at her. This upbeat story provides a glimpse at three generations of an urban family. (Ages 4–8)

Greenfield, Eloise, and Alesia Revis. *Alesia.* Illustrated by George Ford and Sandra Turner Bond. New York: Putnam, Philomel, 1981. 80 pages.

This true story, based on passages from the journal of a teenager with a disability, provide insight into her daily problems, hopes, and concerns. Alesia was partially paralyzed when she was hit by a car at age nine. The entries span the eight months prior to her eighteenth birthday. (Ages 12 and older)

Grimes, Nikki. *Something on My Mind.* Illustrated by Tom Feelings. New York: Dial Books, 1986. 32 pages.

Sensitive drawings illustrate these prose poems that reflect the thoughts and feelings of African-American children growing up. (Ages 5 and older)

Guy, Rosa. *The Friends.* New York: Bantam, 1983. 208 pages.

After Phyllisia and her family move from the West Indies to Harlem, she must cope with the prejudices of her classmates, who think she "talks funny," and with her own attitudes toward the one person who is friendly—an outspoken girl from an impoverished family. (Ages 12 and older)

————. *Paris, Pee Wee, and Big Dog.* Illustrated by Caroline Binch. New York: Delacorte, 1985. 112 pages.

It's Saturday morning, and even though Paris is supposed to be cleaning the apartment while his mother works, he cannot resist roller-skating with his friends. Their adventures soon lead to trouble in this heartwarming story. (Ages 9–12)

————. *The Ups and Downs of Carl Davis III.* New York: Delacorte, 1989. 128 pages.

While visiting his grandmother's home in South Carolina, 12-year-old Carl writes letters to his parents in New York City. In this funny but serious novel, Carl's letters reveal why all people need to know African-American history in order to better understand contemporary American life. (Ages 10 and older)

Hamilton, Virginia. *Sweet Whispers, Brother Rush.* New York: Putnam, Philomel, 1982. 224 pages.

In this creative story about family relationships, 14-year-old Tree, who resents having to run the household and care for her brother when her working mother is away, comes to a better understanding of herself and of her family when she meets the ghost of her uncle, Brother Rush. (Ages 11 and older)

————. *M.C. Higgins, the Great.* New York: Macmillan, Collier, 1987. 288 pages.

A young boy learns more about himself, his heritage, and his environment as he tries to save his mountain home. (Ages 12 and older)

————. *Cousins.*   New York: Putnam, Philomel, 1990.   128 pages.

This powerful novel about a family crisis describes a young person's sorrow at the death of her cousin. The book focuses on the girl's special relationship with her grandmother, who helps her work through her grief.   (Ages 8–12)

Hansen, Joyce.   *The Gift-Giver.*   New York: Ticknor & Fields, Clarion Books, 1989.   128 pages.

This story of young friendship is set in a busy, thriving New York City neighborhood. Ten-year-old Doris has strict parents, whose love for her is shown by their concerns and rules. The author skillfully uses modified black English to tell the story. (Ages 9–13)

————. *Yellow Bird and Me.*   New York: Ticknor & Fields, Clarion Books, 1986.   160 pages.

This sequel to *The Gift-Giver* stands on its own as a story of friendship and loyalty. Doris becomes better acquainted with a classmate whom she has always regarded as annoying. The characterizations of both Doris and Yellow Bird are handled well, and the illustrations are skillfully drawn. Modified black English is used in both the dialogue and the narrative. (Ages 9–13)

Hoffman, Mary.   *Amazing Grace.*   Illustrated by Caroline Binch. New York: Dial Books, 1991.   32 pages.

One of Grace's favorite things to do is to act out stories, putting herself in the best parts. With a creative imagination and household items for props, she becomes Joan of Arc, Anansi the Spider, Hiawatha, and Aladdin. She explores lost kingdoms, sails the seven seas, and cures people who are sick. When she has the chance to play Peter Pan in the school play, Grace learns that she really can be anything she wants to be, despite the doubts of others.   (Ages 4–7)

Hopkins, Lee B.   *A Song in Stone: City Poems.*   Illustrated by Anna Held Audette.   New York: Harper & Row, T.Y. Crowell, 1983. 48 pages.

The 20 short poems in this collection focus on the city. Among the works included are poems by Maxine Kumin, Ruth Krauss,

Langston Hughes, and Norma Farber. Black-and-white photographs underscore the collection's themes.   (Ages 4–11)

Howard, Elizabeth Fitzgerald.   *The Train to Lulu's.*   Illustrated by Robert Casilla.   New York: Macmillan, Bradbury Press, 1988. 32 pages.

Set in the 1930s, this first-person narrative tells the story of two young sisters who travel by train from Boston to Baltimore. Independent and self-reliant as travelers, the sisters are to spend the summer with their grandmother Lulu. Watercolor paintings help convey the anticipation, boredom, and excitement of the girls' nine-hour trip.   (Ages 4–8)

————. *Aunt Flossie's Hats (and Crab Cakes Later).*   Illustrated by James Ransome.   New York: Houghton Mifflin, Clarion Books, 1991.   32 pages.

During their weekly Sunday afternoon visit, two girls enjoy a tea party with their Aunt Flossie and try on her many hats. Each hat is accompanied by a story, most of which involve the history of African Americans in Baltimore. The illustrator's rich oil paintings capture the warm relationship that Aunt Flossie and her grandnieces share.   (Ages 4–8)

Hudson, Cheryl W., and Bernette G. Ford.   *Bright Eyes, Brown Skin.* Illustrated by George Ford.   Orange, N.J.: Just Us Books, 1990. 24 pages.

The simple rhyming text and bright illustrations showing African-American children brimming with confidence as they enjoy the activities of a typical school day make this inviting picture book a delight to read.   (Ages 4–5)

Hudson, Wade.   *Jamal's Busy Day.*   Illustrated by George Ford. Orange, N.J.: Just Us Books, 1991.   24 pages.

This engaging picture book parallels the daily labors of a child named Jamal and his parents, both of whom are active, serious professionals. As readers follow the events in Jamal's school day and in his parents' work day, they discover several upbeat messages—that hard work leads to accomplishments for both children and parents, that all people have something to contribute, and that all work has value.   (Ages 6–8)

Hughes, Langston. *Dream Keeper and Other Poems.* Illustrated by Helen Sewell. New York: Alfred A. Knopf, 1986. 77 pages.

These sensitive poems, favorites of young people for many years, remain appealing for their celebration of African-American culture and their vivid portrayal of the hopes and dreams of youth. Fifty-nine poems are presented, including lyrical poems, songs, and blues. (Ages 12 and older)

Hunter, Kristin. *The Soul Brothers and Sister Lou.* New York: Avon, Flare, 1976. 192 pages.

A 14-year-old girl searches for ways to pursue her dreams amidst the harsh realities of ghetto life. (Ages 12 and older)

Johnson, Angela. *Tell Me a Story, Mama.* Illustrated by David Soman. New York: Orchard, 1989. 32 pages.

A young child listens to her mother's true bedtime stories about her own childhood. The author draws readers into the warm family memories of past comings and goings, partings and reunions. A superb presentation of intergenerational ties is created through a question-and-answer dialogue. The detailed watercolor paintings will appeal to young children. (Ages 3–9)

———. *Do Like Kyla.* Illustrated by James Ransome. New York: Orchard, 1990. 32 pages.

A young girl follows her older sister Kyla everywhere, watching and imitating everything she does. One day the younger sister gets her own chance to lead. Oil paintings illustrate this warm story of two loving sisters. (Ages 3–5)

———. *When I Am Old with You.* Illustrated by David Soman. New York: Orchard, 1990. 32 pages.

A young boy imagines a time when he will be old with his Grandaddy and will sit beside him in a rocking chair and talk about everything—just as they do now. Lovely, rich watercolors enhance the feelings of warmth and love shared by a grandfather and his grandson. (Ages 3–7)

———. *One of Three.* Illustrated by David Soman. New York: Orchard, 1991. 32 pages.

The strength and love of family relationships is presented in this warm, simple story narrated by the youngest of three sisters. The child thinks of herself as one of three when she is with her two sisters, and as one of three when she is with her mother and father. (Ages 3–5)

Johnson, Herschel. *A Visit to the Country.* Illustrated by Romare Bearden. New York: Harper & Row, 1989. 32 pages.

While visiting his grandparents in the country, young Mike finds and cares for an injured baby cardinal until the bird is ready to live independently once again. The full-color paintings that illustrate this touching story are the only works by the late Romare Bearden to appear in a children's book. (Ages 3–6)

Jonas, Ann. *The Quilt.* New York: Greenwillow, 1984. 32 pages.

As a young girl searches in her sleep for a stuffed toy that fell off her bed, scenes depicted on the girl's patchwork quilt come to life in a series of dream images. Bold, full-color illustrations dramatize the interplay between dreams and reality in this original, creative work. (Ages 3–6)

———. *The Trek.* New York: William Morrow, Mulberry, 1989. 32 pages.

As two young friends walk to school one morning through a make-believe "jungle," they see all kinds of wild animals in the shapes of rocks, bushes, trees, and buildings. Readers will delight in finding the animals for themselves. (Ages 3–9)

Mathis, Sharon Bell. *The Hundred Penny Box.* Illustrated by Leo and Diane Dillon. New York: Puffin, 1986. 48 pages.

One of Michael's favorite things to do is to sit with Aunt Dew and count pennies from her hundred penny box. There are 100 pennies in the box—one for each of Aunt Dew's birthdays. As Michael counts, Aunt Dew tells the story behind each penny. When Michael's mother wants to throw away the hundred penny box, Michael decides to try to save the box, and the stories of Aunt Dew's life. This touching novel tells of the love between a young boy and his elderly aunt. (Ages 6–9)

———. *Sidewalk Story.* Illustrated by Leo Carty. New York: Puffin, 1986. 64 pages.

In this powerful story, Lilly Etta tries to help save her friend's belongings after Tanya and her family are evicted and their possessions left out on the sidewalk. (Ages 7–11)

————. *Teacup Full of Roses.* New York: Puffin, 1987. 125 pages.

This poignant story focuses on drug abuse and its effects on one family. (Ages 8–12)

McKissack, Patricia C. *Mirandy and Brother Wind.* Illustrated by Jerry Pinkney. New York: Alfred A. Knopf, 1988. 32 pages.

In this story set in the rural South during the early twentieth century, Mirandy overlooks an obvious partner for her first cakewalk as she tries to find Brother Wind. The book's colorful, appealing illustrations complement the narrative. The author explains the African-American origins of the cakewalk in a brief autobiographical note. (Ages 4–8)

McKissack, Patricia C., and Frederick McKissack. *Taking a Stand against Racism and Racial Discrimination.* New York: Franklin Watts, 1990. 157 pages.

Among the topics covered in this examination of racism in the United States are forms of racism, government policy toward racism, and effective ways to battle racial injustice. One chapter addresses name-calling, racial slurs, and derogatory jokes. An extensive bibliography, detailed source notes, and an index make this an invaluable resource. (Ages 11–14)

Mendez, Phil. *The Black Snowman.* Illustrated by Carole Byard. New York: Scholastic, Blue Ribbon Books, 1991. 48 pages.

Jacob, an angry and bitter child, associates his family's poverty with their race. Reluctantly, Jacob joins his younger brother's efforts to build a snowman from the city's traffic-dirtied snow. The rag the boys find and drape over the snowman is actually a colorful West African Kente cloth. Its magical powers enable Jacob to envision the majesty of his ancient African ancestors. (Ages 7–10)

Moore, Emily. *Whose Side Are You On?* New York: Farrar, Straus & Giroux, Sunburst Books, 1990. 128 pages.

Barbara befriends pesky T.J., the sixth grader who is assigned to tutor her in math. When Barbara learns more about T.J., she tries to rectify what she thinks is an injustice. (Ages 11–14)

————. *Something to Count On.* New York: Puffin, 1991. 112 pages.

Although Lorraine's parents divorce, she is able to balance her feelings of disappointment and frustration with the warmth and companionship of new friendships. This is a satisfying story about relationships in an urban African-American family. (Ages 10–12)

Myers, Walter Dean. *Motown and Didi: A Love Story.* New York: Viking, 1984. 192 pages.

Despite the temptation to look the other way, the independent-minded Motown defends Didi from a gang of thugs who confront her after she reports a group of drug dealers to the police. The two Harlem teenagers join forces in a dangerous fight against the pushers whose drugs are destroying Didi's brother. (Ages 13 and older)

————. *Fast Sam, Cool Clyde, and Stuff.* New York: Puffin, 1988. 192 pages.

Memories of a year in the life of a Harlem youth are the focus of this bittersweet novel. (Ages 10 and older)

————. *Me, Mop and the Moondance Kid.* Illustrated by Rodney Pate. New York: Delacorte, 1988. 128 pages.

Two brothers are adopted into a loving African-American family living in an integrated urban neighborhood. This memorable story, set against the backdrop of the boys' experiences on a baseball team, focuses on a boy who does not play baseball well but never gives up on himself. (Ages 7–11)

————. *The Young Landlords.* New York: Puffin, 1989. 208 pages.

During their summer vacation Paul and his friends from the Action Group find themselves serving as the landlords of an apartment building. They enjoy the fun until the responsibility of managing a building hits home with cranky tenants, endless repairs, and accusations of theft. Despite the problems, the friends try to make their Harlem neighborhood a better place to live. (Ages 9–12)

Ringgold, Faith. *Tar Beach.* Illustrated by Faith Ringgold. New York: Crown, 1991. 32 pages.

The story in this creative picture book originated with a scene from the author's own story quilt. A patch in the quilt depicts a Harlem rooftop at night with four adults playing cards and two children lying on a blanket nearby, gazing at the stars. Based on this scene, the author builds a story in which one of the children imagines that she is flying over the city, wearing a bridge for a necklace, giving a building to her father as a present, and visiting an ice cream factory. Superb illustrations complement the theme of childhood innocence. (Ages 4–8)

Serfozo, Mary. *Rain Talk.* Illustrated by Keiko Narahashi. New York: Macmillan, McElderry, 1990. 32 pages.

The sense of wonder experienced by a young girl as she walks in a gentle rain is beautifully expressed by watercolor illustrations and a short, onomatopoeic narrative. (Ages 2–6)

Shelby, Anne. *We Keep a Store.* Illustrated by John Ward. New York: Orchard, 1990. 32 pages.

A young girl helps her family run a country store, which serves as an informal intergenerational community center throughout the seasons of the year. (Ages 4–7)

Springer, Nancy. *They're All Named Wildfire.* New York: Macmillan, Atheneum, 1989. 128 pages.

In this novel of racism and friendship set in rural Pennsylvania, two girls find they cannot ignore the bigotry of others. When Shanterey, who is black, is forbidden to ride a neighbor's horse, Jenny befriends her and suddenly finds herself the target of ridicule at school. (Ages 9 and older)

Steptoe, John. *Stevie.* Illustrated by John Steptoe. New York: Harper & Row, Trophy, 1986. 32 pages.

Robert quickly grows to resent a young boarder named Stevie, who has moved into Robert's home. Stevie tags along everywhere, breaks toys, and gets into trouble. But when Stevie moves away, Robert begins to think that he was not so bad after all. (Ages 3–8)

Stolz, Mary. *Storm in the Night.* Illustrated by Pat Cummings. New York: Harper & Row, Trophy, 1990. 32 pages.

A grandfather and grandson spend a rainy summer night together in their house. When the electrical power fails, young Thomas grows anxious. Grandfather's lively recollections about his own childhood fears help Thomas to overcome his worries. (Ages 4–8)

————. *Go Fish.* Illustrated by Pat Cummings. New York: HarperCollins, 1991. 80 pages.

Thomas and Grandfather share many things during the course of a day, including the stories Grandfather tells him. These stories, which Grandfather first heard from his own grandfather, help Thomas understand his connection to the past and to the future. (Ages 7–11)

Tate, Eleanora E. *The Secret of Gumbo Grove.* New York: Bantam, Starfire, 1988. 256 pages.

Eleven-year-old Raisin volunteers to help an older woman clean up a neglected church cemetery in Gumbo Grove. In the process, they uncover some local African-American history. (Ages 11–14)

————. *Thank You, Dr. Martin Luther King, Jr.!* New York: Franklin Watts, 1990. 237 pages.

Another in the author's series about Gumbo Grove, this novel features a young girl named Mary Elouise, who gains new insights into her heritage from her grandmother and a visiting storyteller. This sensitive book examines racial issues directly and effectively, using true-to-life portrayals. (Ages 9–12)

Thomas, Joyce Carol. *Marked by Fire.* New York: Avon, Flare, 1982. 160 pages.

From the time of her birth in the cotton fields with all the women of the town participating, Abby was a special child to the people of her rural Oklahoma community. Their love and support help the young girl through a painful adolescence, in which she survives a tornado and a physical assault. Her neighbors continue to nurture Abby as she learns her grandmother's gifts of medicine and begins to add her own strength to the community. (Ages 13 and older)

————. *The Golden Pasture.* New York: Scholastic, 1987. 144 pages.

Twelve-year-old Carl Lee spends the summer on the Oklahoma ranch of his grandfather, a former rider on the black rodeo circuit. Amidst all the activity centering on horseback riding, his grandfather's cowhand stories, and the upcoming rodeo, Carl Lee begins to understand the long-standing rift between his father and his grandfather. (Ages 10–14)

Walker, Alice. *Finding the Green Stone.* Illustrated by Catherine Deeter. San Diego: Harcourt Brace Jovanovich, 1991. 40 pages.

Everyone in Johnny's town has a glowing, green stone. Johnny has one too—until he loses it after misbehaving. Johnny searches everywhere for his stone. He soon discovers, however, that he can find it only after searching his own heart. (Ages 7–9)

Walter, Mildred Pitts. *My Mama Needs Me.* Illustrated by Pat Cummings. New York: Lothrop, Lee & Shepard, 1983. 32 pages.

This warm story explores the changes that take place in a family after the birth of a new baby. At first the family's older child, Jason, feels left out and alone. But a chance to help bathe the baby, plus a hug from his mother, help Jason understand that he is still needed and loved. (Ages 4–6)

————. *Trouble's Child.* New York: Lothrop, Lee & Shepard, 1985. 128 pages.

Martha yearns to leave her village and finish high school, but her family's expectations for her future stand in the way. Grandmother Titay, the midwife and healer in their Louisiana island village, wants to pass on her knowledge and her role in the community to Martha. Even Martha's friends urge her to accept her destiny. (Ages 10 and older)

————. *Justin and the Best Biscuits in the World.* Illustrated by Catherine Stock. New York: Alfred A. Knopf, Bullseye Books, 1990. 128 pages.

Justin spends the summer on Grandpa's ranch in Kansas and learns many things. He learns about the racist acts endured by African-American cowhands of the past. He watches Grandpa and learns that men can do household chores. Male and female stereotypes dissolve in this easy-to-read novel about family ties, family heritage, and African-American history. Black-and-white pencil drawings illustrate the book.   (Ages 8–12)

————.   *Mariah Loves Rock.*   Illustrated by Pat Cummings. Mahwah, N.J.: Troll Associates, 1989.   128 pages.

Eleven-year-old Mariah was feeling both excited and nervous. It seemed that when she wasn't thinking about an upcoming appearance by her favorite rock star, she was thinking about what would happen when her father's oldest daughter from his first marriage moved in. This easy-to-read book clearly conveys the emotions of a loving family coping with change. (Ages 8–11)

Wilkinson, Brenda.   *Ludell.*   New York: HarperCollins, 1992. 176 pages.

Ten-year-old Ludell Wilson loves her home in Waycross, Georgia. But as she grows older and more mature, she begins to think more about life outside her hometown. This story, the first in the author's series about Ludell, captures the experiences of a young girl growing up.   (Ages 10 and older)

————.   *Ludell and Willie.*   New York: Bantam, 1985.   144 pages.

Now a teenager, Ludell experiences events that change the plans she and her boyfriend, Willie, have for the future. (Ages 13 and older)

————.   *Ludell's New York Time.*   New York: HarperCollins, 1980. 192 pages.

When Ludell moves from Georgia to New York, she must adjust to living in a big city and to being apart from Willie.   (Ages 13 and older)

Williams, Vera B.   *Cherries and Cherry Pits.*   New York: William Morrow, Mulberry, 1991.   40 pages.

A young girl named Bidemmi tells stories and draws pictures about four people she observes in her urban neighborhood. Each story celebrates human diversity, yet each is ultimately linked by common experience. With stunning watercolor paintings, the author succeeds in communicating on two levels simultaneously—hers and the child's she is depicting. (Ages 4–9)

Wilson, Beth P. *Jenny.* Illustrated by Dolores Johnson. New York: Macmillan, 1990. 32 pages.

This upbeat portrait of a young girl uses a series of brief first-person vignettes to describe her family, friends, experiences, likes, and dislikes. (Ages 5–8)

Woodson, Jacqueline. *Last Summer with Maizon.* New York: Doubleday, 1990. 105 pages.

Two inseparable 11-year-olds, Margaret and Maizon, try to imagine how their lives will change after Maizon leaves their Brooklyn neighborhood to attend a private school, where she expects to be the only African-American student. When Margaret's father dies unexpectedly and she experiences the crushing sense of loss, her dependency on Maizon becomes clear. (Ages 10–13)

Yarbrough, Camille. *Cornrows.* Illustrated by Carole Byard. New York: Putnam, Coward-McCann, 1981. 48 pages.

As they braid each other's hair, Sister and her brother listen to Mama and Great-Grammaw tell the story of the art of cornrowing. (Ages 7–11)

————. *The Shimmershine Queens.* New York: Alfred A. Knopf, Bullseye Books, 1990. 144 pages.

Great-cousin Seatta imparts her strength and wisdom to help fifth-grader Angie overcome problems at home and at school. As Angie learns the importance of the past and of always doing her best, her self-esteem grows. Pride in the African-American heritage is the central theme of this finely crafted urban novel. (Ages 8–12)

The Past

Berleth, Richard. *Samuel's Choice.* Illustrated by James Watling. Morton Grove, Ill.: Whitman, 1990. 40 pages.

This fictional account, which details the Battle of Long Island and General Washington's miraculous retreat to Manhattan, focuses on the contributions of a 14-year-old Brooklyn slave. (Ages 8–11)

Feelings, Tom. *Tommy Traveller in the World of Black History.*
Illustrated by Tom Feelings. New York: Writers & Readers, 1991.
48 pages.

A young boy named Tommy becomes friends with a
neighborhood doctor, who invites him to browse in his library.
Tommy's reading transports him to the past, where he meets
Phoebe Frances, Emmet Till, Aesop, Frederick Douglass, Crispus
Attucks, and Joe Louis. The comic-book style illustrations make
this introduction to African-American history especially
appealing. (Ages 7–11)

Fleischman, Paul. *The Borning Room.* New York: HarperCollins,
1991. 80 pages.

The borning room, commonly located off the kitchen in early
American homes and reserved for births, illnesses, and deaths,
serves as a focal point in this first-person narrative about the life
of Georgina Lott. As the story follows Georgina at different
stages in her life, it provides readers with a glimpse of
nineteenth-century America and the injustices of slavery.
(Ages 11 and older)

Freedman, Russell. *Children of the Wild West.* New York:
Houghton Mifflin, Clarion Books, 1990. 128 pages.

Historical photographs with an accompanying narrative
document the lives of young European Americans, African
Americans, Native Americans, and Asian Americans growing up
in the American West during the nineteenth century. Frontier
schools, wagon trains, and celebrations are pictured and
described—all from a child's perspective. (Ages 7 and older)

Hamilton, Virginia. *Willie Bea and the Time the Martians Landed.*
New York: Macmillan, Aladdin, 1989. 224 pages.

In rural Ohio during late October 1938, Willie Bea and her family
become caught up in two days of confusion and fear caused
by Orson Welles's celebrated radio broadcast, *The War of the
Worlds.* With insight and humor, Hamilton brilliantly recreates
another time and place. (Ages 9 and older)

———. *The House of Dies Drear.* Illustrated by Eros Keith. New
York: Macmillan, Collier Books, 1984. 256 pages.

When Thomas Small moves with his family to Ohio, he learns that
his new house was once a station on the Underground Railroad.

Thomas also learns that the house, built by abolitionist Dies Drear, holds many secrets. As Thomas searches for answers to those secrets, he discovers a deeper sense of his own connection to the past.   (Ages 11 and older)

————. *The Mystery of Drear House: The Conclusion of the Dies Drear Chronicle.*   New York: Macmillan, Collier Books, 1988. 224 pages.

Abolitionist Dies Drear's magnificent treasure has been uncovered, and Thomas Small and his family must decide on the best way to keep it safe. In this absorbing story, readers meet two unforgettable characters, Thomas's great-grandmother and his neighbor, both of whom remember a wealth of history. (Ages 11 and older)

Katz, William L.   *Breaking the Chains: African-American Slave Resistance.*   New York: Macmillan, Atheneum, 1990.   194 pages.

A fascinating array of oral histories, newspaper reports, and public records document the many ways in which enslaved people resisted oppression. Black-and-white photographs and illustrations help convey the powerful impact of slave defiance and courage.   (Ages 12 and older)

Lester, Julius.   *This Strange New Feeling.*   New York: Scholastic, 1985.   164 pages.

Three moving love stories based on true events convey the impact of slavery on the human spirit.   (Ages 13 and older)

————. *To Be a Slave.*   Illustrated by Tom Feelings.   New York: Scholastic, 1986.   160 pages.

This powerful narrative history presents the personal accounts of former slaves and the horrors they suffered.   (Ages 13 and older)

Little, Lessie Jones.   *Children of Long Ago: Poems.*   Illustrated by Jan Spivey Gilchrist.   New York: Putnam, Philomel, 1988. 32 pages.

Seventeen poems by Lessie Jones Little, the mother of poet and fiction writer Eloise Greenfield, evoke the poet's memories of family life in rural North Carolina in the early 1900s. Full-color illustrations enhance the stories told.   (Ages 3–9)

Marie, D. *Tears for Ashan.* Illustrated by Norman Childers. Memphis: Creative Press Works, 1989. 32 pages.

An African boy grieves when his best friend is kidnapped by slave traders and taken away in a big ship. Cultural details and emotional expression are combined in this account of a painful period of history told from the African perspective. (Ages 7–11)

McKissack, Patricia C., and Frederick McKissack. *The Civil Rights Movement in America from 1865 to the Present.* Chicago: Childrens Press, 1987. 320 pages.

This historical overview identifies many of the people who were important to the civil rights movement—including men and women whose efforts in the 1950s and 1960s may not have received appropriate recognition. Black-and-white illustrations accompany the narrative, and capsule summaries highlighting people, organizations, and events offer a handy additional reference. (Ages 12 and older)

————. *A Long Hard Journey: The Story of the Pullman Porter.* New York: Walker, 1990. 144 pages.

This history of the African-American porters who worked aboard George Pullman's luxury sleeping cars is thorough and well researched. From the first generation of porters emancipated from slavery to those who organized a union under the leadership of A. Philip Randolph, the book chronicles the heroic struggles for improved working conditions, better pay, and fair treatment. (Ages 11 and older)

Meltzer, Milton. *All Times, All Peoples: A World History of Slavery.* Illustrated by Leonard Everett Fisher. New York: Harper & Row, 1980. 80 pages.

This tragic history of enslaved people shows that human bondage has existed among many societies and cultures throughout the world since earliest recorded time. The book contains many black-and-white drawings. (Ages 9 and older)

————. *The Black Americans: A History in Their Own Words, 1619–1983.* Rev. ed. New York: Harper & Row, T.Y. Crowell, 1984. 320 pages.

Speeches, letters, eyewitness accounts, court testimony, and other primary-source materials offer a social history of the

African-American experience. Each item is introduced by a note identifying the speaker or writer and the historical context or setting. (Ages 12 and older)

————. *Underground Man.* San Diego: Harcourt Brace Jovanovich, Gulliver Books, 1990. 288 pages.

Nineteen-year-old Josh Bowen follows his conscience and becomes a conductor on the Underground Railroad, an act that eventually leads to his arrest, trial, and imprisonment. Inspired by a true story, this exciting novel tells of courage in the face of great danger. (Ages 8–11)

Moore, Yvette. *Freedom Songs.* New York: Orchard, 1991. 176 pages.

In this first-person narrative set in the 1960s, Sheryl and her family leave their comfortable Brooklyn home for an Easter visit with Sheryl's grandmother in North Carolina. After experiencing the blatant realities of Jim Crow racism and learning about the dangerous Freedom Rides undertaken by her uncle, Sheryl is determined to help her people. (Ages 12 and older)

Myers, Walter Dean. *Fallen Angels.* New York: Scholastic, 1989. 336 pages.

This gripping novel focuses on the experiences of five young men serving in Vietnam. Their powerful, heartbreaking story, told by a 17-year-old soldier named Richie Perry, reveals the human consequences of war. (Ages 13 and older)

————. *Now Is Your Time! The African-American Struggle for Freedom.* New York: HarperCollins, Trophy, 1991. 320 pages.

This sweeping history presents the quests and struggles of individual African Americans against the background of broader historical movements. Through the accounts of freed slave Ibrahima, investigative reporter Ida Wells, artist Meta Warrick Fuller, inventor George Latimore, the soldiers of the 54th Massachusetts Regiment, and others, readers gain a deeper understanding of past and present. (Ages 11 and older)

O'Dell, Scott. *My Name Is Not Angelica.* Boston: Houghton Mifflin, 1989. 144 pages.

In this moving historical novel, 16-year-old Raisha is snatched from her home in Africa and forced aboard a slave ship bound for St. John Island in the West Indies. Later, while held as a house slave on a Danish plantation, Raisha joins in the daring slave revolt of 1733 and 1734.   (Ages 10–14)

Sterne, Emma G.   *The Slave Ship.*   Illustrated by David Lockhart. New York: Scholastic, 1988.   192 pages.

The *Amistad,* a slave ship carrying Africans kidnapped from their homes, is the setting of this true story about the triumph of right over might. During their forced journey, the Africans manage to free themselves, commandeer the ship, and sail it to the northeast coast of the United States. Their fate eventually is decided by the Supreme Court, which rules that the Africans should be freed.   (Ages 12 and older)

Taylor, Mildred D.   *Song of the Trees.*   Illustrated by Jerry Pinkney. New York: Dial Books, 1985.   56 pages.

This touching novel is the first in the author's highly acclaimed series about a young African-American girl named Cassie Logan and her family. Set in the South during the Great Depression, Cassie's father leads the fight to save the trees surrounding the family's Mississippi home.   (Ages 7–10)

————.   *Roll of Thunder, Hear My Cry.*   New York: Dial Books, 1976. 276 pages.

During one turbulent year Cassie's safe and secure world is turned upside down as she experiences the fear and confusion of racism. Set in the South during the 1930s, this unforgettable novel tells of courage, survival, and the love and strength of family.   (Ages 11 and older)

————.   *Let the Circle Be Unbroken.*   New York: Bantam, 1983. 432 pages.

The Logans and their neighbors draw closer together as they face prejudice and poverty in rural Mississippi during the Great Depression.   (Ages 12 and older)

————.   *The Friendship.*   Illustrated by Max Ginsburg.   New York: Dial Books, 1987.   56 pages.

The Logan children witness racism firsthand during a frightening scene at the general store. A respected community elder dares to call the white store owner by his first name and is attacked by a group of white men. The strength, courage, and dignity of Mr. Tom Bee offer a memorable African-American role model. (Ages 9–14)

————. *The Gold Cadillac.*   Illustrated by Michael Hays.   New York: Dial Books, 1987.   48 pages.

A young girl and her sister are thrilled when their father buys a new gold Cadillac, despite the feelings of confusion brought by Mother's disapproval. But excitement and pride turn to tension and fear as the family and their splendid new car are met with suspicion and anger on a trip south to visit relatives. Set in the 1950s, this poignant story vividly describes both the strength of family and the horrors of racism as seen through the eyes of a child.   (Ages 9–13)

————. *Mississippi Bridge.*   Illustrated by Max Ginsburg.   New York: Dial Books, 1990.   64 pages.

Ten-year-old Jeremy Simms stands on the front steps of a store in a small Mississippi town in the 1930s. He watches as the weekly bus pulls in to load passengers and luggage. As white passengers begin to fill up the seats, the black passengers are ordered off the bus. Jeremy, who is white, sees the unfairness in the situation, but he remains silent. Interracial tensions and interactions are flawlessly depicted in this gripping story, which builds to a dramatic, surprising conclusion.   (Ages 9–13)

————. *The Road to Memphis.*   New York: Dial Books, 1990. 240 pages.

It is 1941 and Cassie Logan is finishing high school and thinking about college and law school. Yet her dreams are put aside for three tense days when she tries to help a young man flee following a racial incident. This story, set against the backdrop of World War II, tells of anger and remorse as well as respect and friendship.   (Ages 13 and older)

Winter, Jeanette.   *Follow the Drinking Gourd.*   New York: Alfred A. Knopf, 1988.   48 pages.

A legendary one-legged sailor named Peg Leg Joe teaches plantation slaves the lyrics to a song that will direct them to the Underground Railroad and freedom in the North. Music, folk art, and historical background enhance this story, which traces one family's flight to freedom.   (Ages 6–9)

Biographies and Autobiographies

Adler, David A. *A Picture Book of Martin Luther King, Jr.* Illustrated by Robert Casilla. New York: Holiday, 1989.   32 pages.

Illustrated with full-color art, this short, easy-to-read biography presents the story of King's life and of the civil rights movement. (Ages 3–9)

Aldred, Lisa. *Thurgood Marshall.*   New York: Chelsea House, 1990. 128 pages.

In 1954 Thurgood Marshall successfully argued against school segregation in the case of *Brown v. the Board of Education.* In 1967 he became the first African American appointed to the United States Supreme Court. This straightforward biography tells his story.   (Ages 10 and older)

Altman, Susan. *Extraordinary Black Americans from Colonial to Contemporary Times.*   Chicago: Childrens Press, 1989. 240 pages.

Footnotes, a one-page bibliography, and an index provide easy access to the wealth of information contained in this collection of 85 biographies. Among those featured are Estevanico, Lucy Teiry Smith, Jean Baptiste Pointe Du Sable, Fannie Lou Hamer, Martin Luther King, Jr., and Toni Morrison. The book also contains brief essays on African-American history as well as the complete texts of several critical documents and speeches.   (Ages 7 and older)

Bentley, Judith. *Archbishop Tutu of South Africa.*   Hillside, N.J.: Enslow Publishers, 1988.   96 pages.

This fascinating biography chronicles the life of the South African civil rights leader, Anglican archbishop, and Nobel laureate. The book focuses on Tutu's nonviolent campaign to end his country's system of apartheid.   (Ages 10–15)

————. *Harriet Tubman.*   New York: Franklin Watts, 1990. 144 pages.

This compelling portrait depicts Harriet Tubman's heroic efforts as a conductor for the Underground Railroad. The book also describes Tubman's less publicized accomplishments as a Civil War spy and as a suffragist.   (Ages 10–15)

Blassingame, Wyatt. *Jim Beckwourth: Black Trapper and Indian Chief.* Illustrated by Herman Vestal. New York: Chelsea House, 1991. 80 pages.

The life story of the famous mountain man who was accepted by the Crow people as a chief is carefully documented in this interesting book. (Ages 7–10)

Blue, Rose, and Corinne J. Naden. *Colin Powell: Straight to the Top.* Brookfield, Conn.: Millbrook Press, 1991. 48 pages.

The son of poor Jamaican immigrants, Colin Powell rose through the ranks of the army to become a four-star general and chairman of the Joint Chiefs of Staff. This insightful book shows children how Powell achieved his success. (Ages 7–9)

Celsi, Teresa. *Rosa Parks and the Montgomery Bus Boycott.* Brookfield, Conn.: Millbrook Press, 1991. 32 pages.

When Rosa Parks refused to give up her seat on a Montgomery, Alabama, bus to a white passenger, she helped spark the civil rights movement. This lively account demonstrates how one person can make a difference. (Ages 7–9)

Collier, James L. *Louis Armstrong: An American Success Story.* New York: Macmillan, 1985. 176 pages.

Although he was shy, uneducated, and poor, Louis Armstrong's musical genius enabled him to become the greatest jazz artist of his time. Armstrong's brilliant trumpet playing and unique singing style made him world famous. (Ages 5–9)

Cwiklik, Robert. *Malcolm X and Black Pride.* Brookfield, Conn.: Millbrook Press, 1991. 32 pages.

This book tells the story of how Malcolm X became the leader of a movement to unite black people throughout the world. (Ages 7–9)

Davis, Burke. *Black Heroes of the American Revolution.* San Diego: Harcourt Brace Jovanovich, 1991. 96 pages.

The African-American soldiers, sailors, spies, scouts, guides, and wagoners whose efforts helped achieve American independence are profiled in this book. Included are such heroes as Crispus Attucks, Edward Hector, Austin Dabney, William Lee, and many others. (Ages 8–12)

Davis, Ossie. *Langston: A Play.* New York: Delacorte, 1982. 144 pages.

In this short drama set in the early 1900s, the poet Langston Hughes visits a rehearsal of one of his plays and uses the actors to recreate scenes from his early life. This play within a play features excerpts from Hughes's poetry. (Ages 12 and older)

————. *Escape to Freedom: A Play about Young Frederick Douglass.* New York: Puffin, 1990. 89 pages.

The five scenes in this play, which includes informal and improvisational stage directions, present episodes from the life of Frederick Douglass—his childhood in a slave cabin, his excitement at learning how to read, his treatment on a plantation, his experiences in Baltimore, and his eventual escape to freedom. (Ages 9–12)

De Veaux, Alexis. *Don't Explain: A Song of Billie Holiday.* New York: Harper & Row, 1980. 160 pages.

The life and times of the jazz singer known as Lady Day are recounted in this long, prose poem. Black-and-white photographs illustrate the story. (Ages 12 and older)

Fax, Elton C. *Seventeen Black Artists.* New York: Dodd, Mead, 1972. 306 pages.

This book describes the work of 17 African-American artists who have made exceptional contributions in such fields as painting, sculpture, and photography. Among those included are Romare Bearden, John Biggers, Elizabeth Catlett, Jacob Lawrence, Norma Morgan, and Charles White. (Ages 13 and older)

Feinberg, Brian. *Nelson Mandela.* New York: Chelsea House, 1991. 84 pages.

The courageous story of the leader of the nationalist movement in South Africa is told in this biography. (Ages 7–10)

Ferris, Jeri. *Walking the Road to Freedom: A Story about Sojourner Truth.* Illustrated by Peter E. Hanson. Minneapolis: Lerner, First Avenue Editions, 1989. 64 pages.

This vivid narrative describes the life of Sojourner Truth as she traveled throughout the United States, calling for freedom and equality for all. (Ages 8–11)

Gilman, Michael. *Matthew Henson.* New York: Chelsea House, 1988. 112 pages.

This remarkable story depicts the vision, accomplishments, courage, and fortitude of Arctic explorer Matthew Henson. (Ages 12 and older)

Haber, Louis. *Black Pioneers of Science and Invention.* San Diego: Harcourt Brace Jovanovich, 1991. 288 pages.

Fourteen African Americans who played significant roles in the scientific and technological progress of the United States are profiled in this highly readable book. The work of some of these inventors had for many years gone unrecognized. Yet their achievements have made the jobs of many Americans easier, saved countless lives, and in some cases changed the course of history. (Ages 8–12)

Hamilton, Virginia. *W.E.B. Du Bois: A Biography.* New York: Harper & Row, T.Y. Crowell, 1987. 192 pages.

The life of the noted historian and activist who helped found the National Association for the Advancement of Colored People (NAACP) is the subject of this fascinating biography. (Ages 10–13)

————. *Anthony Burns: The Defeat and Triumph of a Fugitive Slave.* New York: Alfred A. Knopf, 1988. 192 pages.

This carefully researched account focuses on Anthony Burns's 1854 Boston trial. The book includes accounts of Burns's imprisonment and trial that are based on actual primary sources as well as innovative fictional segments that highlight his youth as an enslaved child in Virginia. (Ages 12 and older)

Hancock, Sibyl. *Famous Firsts of Black Americans.* Illustrated by Jerry Haynes. Bretna, La.: Pelican, 1983. 128 pages.

This collection of brief biographical sketches includes profiles of such figures as Phillis Wheatley, Charles Richard Drew, and Richard Allen. (Ages 8–14)

Haskins, James. *Barbara Jordan.* New York: Dial Books, 1977. 215 pages.

Barbara Jordan, the first African-American woman from a Southern state to be elected to the United States Congress, devoted her life to public service. This straightforward account chronicles the life and political career of this highly respected role model.   (Ages 10 and older)

————. *The Story of Stevie Wonder.*   New York: Dell, 1979. 128 pages.

This biography tells the story of a child prodigy who overcame adversity to become a Grammy-Award-winning composer, pianist, and singer.   (Ages 10 and older)

————. *Lena Horne.*   New York: Putnam, Coward-McCann, 1983. 160 pages.

The singer and actress who developed a distinctive vocal style and achieved international fame is the subject of this inspiring biography.   (Ages 11 and older)

————. *Bill Cosby: America's Most Famous Father.*   New York: Walker, 1988.   128 pages.

Internationally known comedian and television star Bill Cosby is the subject of this engaging biography.   (Ages 12 and older)

Haskins, James, and Kathleen Benson.   *Space Challenger: The Story of Guion Bluford.*   Minneapolis: Carolrhoda Books, 1984. 64 pages.

As a child growing up in Philadelphia, Guion Bluford dreamed of being an astronaut and traveling in space. On August 30, 1983, his dream came true. This intriguing biography details the life of the first African American to travel in space.   (Ages 8–11)

Hudson, Wade, and Valerie W. Wesley.   *Afro-Bets Book of Black Heroes from A to Z: An Introduction to Important Black Achievers for Young Readers.*   Orange, N.J.: Just Us Books, 1988. 64 pages.

Fifty-one historical and contemporary black men and women, including Mary McLeod Bethune, Matthew Henson, Jesse Jackson, Zora Neale Hurston, Thurgood Marshall, Kwame Nkrumrah, Wilma Rudolph, Sojourner Truth, Leslie Uggams, and Shaka Zulu, are featured in this collection of one-page biographies. Black-and-white photographs as well as creative illustrations enhance the biographies.   (Ages 5–11)

Humphrey, Kathryn L. *Satchel Paige.* New York: Franklin Watts, 1988. 128 pages.

This biography of the famous baseball player offers readers insights into a time in American society when professional baseball teams were not integrated—a time when players had to stay on their side of the "color line," no matter how great their skills. (Ages 12 and older)

Igus, Toyomi, ed. *Book of Black Heroes: Great Women in the Struggle.* Orange, N.J.: Just Us Books, 1991. 96 pages.

This volume focuses on the achievements of 84 black women in world history, chronicling both their struggles and their successes as they worked to improve the lives of their people. The book is divided into eight main parts: Freedom Fighters, Educators, Writers and Fine Artists, Performing Artists, Athletes, Entrepreneurs, Lawyers and Policy Makers, and Scientists and Healers. (Ages 9–13)

Katz, William L. *Black People Who Made the Old West.* New York: Harper & Row, T.Y. Crowell, 1989. 160 pages.

This collection of biographical sketches provides readers with lively descriptions and amusing anecdotes about 35 African-American men and women of the western frontier. (Ages 12 and older)

Klots, Steve. *Richard Allen: Religious Leader and Social Activist.* New York: Chelsea House, 1991. 112 pages.

This book details the life of Richard Allen, the founder of the African Methodist Episcopal Church and a leader of the African-American community in post-Revolutionary Philadelphia. (Ages 10 and older)

Larsen, Rebecca. *Paul Robeson: Hero before His Time.* New York: Franklin Watts, 1989. 158 pages.

This thoroughly researched biography chronicles the life and work of the actor, singer, and political activist. Black-and-white photographs illustrate the narrative. (Ages 11 and older)

Lyons, Mary E. *Sorrow's Kitchen: The Life and Folklore of Zora Neale Hurston.* New York: Macmillan, Charles Scribner's, 1990. 160 pages.

Growing up in the all-black town of Eatonville, Florida, Zora Neale Hurston delighted in hearing the oral folk literature of her people. As an adult, she gave their oral literature the scholarly attention it deserved. Hurston's struggles to gain an education and to have her research taken seriously, her role as a creative artist in the Harlem Renaissance, and her lifelong commitment to preserving the cultural heritage of African Americans are carefully documented in this stirring biography. (Ages 11 and older)

Mathis, Sharon Bell. *Ray Charles.* Illustrated by George Ford. New York: Harper & Row, T.Y. Crowell, 1973. 32 pages.

The inspiring story of the great pianist and jazz singer who overcame many difficulties to achieve fame in the music world is told in this biography. (Ages 8–11)

McKissack, Patricia C. *Mary McLeod Bethune: A Great American Educator.* Chicago: Childrens Press, 1985. 111 pages.

This moving tribute to Bethune's celebrated career traces her life as a reader, student, teacher, dreamer, builder, crusader, college president, and presidential adviser. Children also will learn about her lasting legacy—Bethune-Cookman College in Daytona Beach, Florida. (Ages 10–13)

————. *Jesse Jackson: A Biography.* New York: Scholastic, 1989. 122 pages.

Tracing the development of Jackson's leadership from spokesperson for black causes to advocate for the disenfranchised, this fast-paced biography provides a balanced presentation of his emergence as a political force in the United States. (Ages 8–12)

McKissack, Patricia C., and Frederick McKissack. *Frederick Douglass: The Black Lion.* Chicago: Childrens Press, 1987. 136 pages.

Frederick Douglass, the self-educated African-American leader who was once enslaved, became a dynamic spokesperson in the antislavery movements of the nineteenth century. An index, chronological biographical information, and occasional black-and-white photographs are useful components of the book. (Ages 9–14)

Milton, Joyce. *Marching to Freedom: The Story of Martin Luther King, Jr.* New York: Dell, Yearling Books, 1987. 92 pages.

Brief excerpts from King's speeches and seven pages of black-and-white photographs enhance this easy-to-read biography. (Ages 9–14)

Patterson, Charles. *Marian Anderson.* New York: Franklin Watts, 1988. 160 pages.

Even as a young girl growing up in Philadelphia, Marian Anderson was recognized as a gifted singer. With the loving support of family and friends, she managed to rise above both poverty and racism to achieve fame doing what she liked to do best—sing. This engaging, readable biography traces the path of Anderson's success. (Ages 12 and older)

Patterson, Lillie. *Dr. Martin Luther King, Jr.: Man of Peace.* Champaign, Ill.: Garrard Press, 1969. 96 pages.

This touching biography tells the story of the renowned minister, orator, and civil rights leader, giving special attention to his philosophy of nonviolence. (Ages 8–10)

Pelz, Ruth. *Black Heroes of the Wild West.* Illustrated by Leandro Della Piana. Seattle: Open Hand, 1989. 57 pages.

This collection of essays chronicles the lives of notable African Americans who helped shape the Western frontier. The book features the achievements of explorers, pioneers, cowhands, and entrepreneurs. (Ages 7–9)

Petry, Ann. *Harriet Tubman: Conductor on the Underground Railroad.* New York: Harper & Row, T.Y. Crowell, 1955. 247 pages.

The story of this courageous abolitionist who risked her life to help others is told in this inspiring biography. (Ages 12 and older)

————. *Tituba of Salem Village.* New York: HarperCollins, Trophy, 1991. 272 pages.

This powerful novel tells the story of Tituba, an enslaved woman from the island of Barbados, whose strength and dignity remained firm despite the terror and superstition that surrounded her during the Salem witchcraft trials.   (Ages 12 and older)

Poitier, Sidney.   *This Life.*   New York: Ballantine, 1981.   416 pages.

Sidney Poitier, the first African-American actor to win an Oscar, takes a look back at his extraordinary life and career.   (Ages 13 and older)

Preston, Kitty.   *Scott Joplin.*   New York: Chelsea House, 1988. 112 pages.

At the turn of the century Scott Joplin was a leading composer of the lively genre of ragtime music. This biography focuses on the career of the gifted musician and on his contributions to American music.   (Ages 10 and older)

Reynolds, Barbara.   *And Still We Rise: Interviews with 50 Black Role Models.*   Washington, D.C.: USA Today Books, 1988.   221 pages.

This collection of newspaper columns focuses on the lives of 50 African Americans who serve as contemporary role models for children. The people profiled come from many different backgrounds and represent a wide range of professions, including church leaders, politicians, business leaders, physicians, entertainment figures, and athletes. Each entry features a background summary, a series of interview questions and answers, a biographical chronology, and a photograph. (Ages 9 and older)

Roberts, Naurice.   *Harold Washington: Mayor with a Vision.* Chicago: Childrens Press, 1988.   30 pages.

This easy-to-read biography of Chicago's first African-American mayor includes a variety of photographs as well as a chronology of Washington's life.   (Ages 7–9)

Robinson, Jackie.   *I Never Had It Made: The Autobiography of Jackie Robinson.*   As told to Alfred Duckett. New York: Putnam, 1972.   230 pages.

This autobiography tells the story of the first African American to play major league baseball in the twentieth century.   (Ages 12 and older)

Rollins, Charlemae H. *Black Troubadour: Langston Hughes.* Chicago: Rand McNally, 1971. 144 pages.

The life of the celebrated author and poet is chronicled in this inspiring biography. (Ages 12 and older)

Scheader, Catherine. *Shirley Chisholm: Teacher and Congresswoman.* Hillside, N.J.: Enslow Publishers, 1990. 128 pages.

The first African-American woman to serve in Congress and the first to run for President of the United States, Shirley Chisholm has devoted her career to public service. This biography focuses on Chisholm's achievements as a teacher and member of Congress and tells how she continues to work today to promote education and to help those in need. (Ages 10 and older)

Schroeder, Alan. *Ragtime Tumpie.* Illustrated by Bernie Fuchs. Boston: Little, Brown, 1989. 32 pages.

The sound of ragtime filled the streets of St. Louis in the early 1900s, inspiring young Tumpie to dream of becoming a famous dancer. Vibrant paintings complement this story of the childhood of Josephine Baker. (Ages 4–9)

Shumate, Jane. *Sojourner Truth and the Voice of Freedom.* Brookfield, Conn.: Millbrook Press, 1991. 32 pages.

Sojourner Truth's travels throughout the United States talking, preaching, and singing about freedom for all people are described in this stirring biography. (Ages 7–9)

Smith, Kathie B. *Martin Luther King, Jr.* Illustrated by James Seward. Englewood Cliffs, N.J.: Julian Messner, 1987. 24 pages.

This easy-to-read biography explains the civil rights movement and details King's leadership within this social revolution. (Ages 6–11)

Stanley, Diane, and Peter Vennema. *Shaka: King of the Zulus.* Illustrated by Diane Stanley. New York: William Morrow, 1988. 40 pages.

This picture book tells the story of the great nineteenth-century Zulu chief. Appealing visuals, a glossary, and a list of sources give children a fascinating introduction to this famous leader's accomplishments. (Ages 5–11)

Tanenhaus, Sam. *Louis Armstrong.* New York: Chelsea House, 1989. 112 pages.

The world-famous musician's difficult, streetwise beginnings and his fascination with jazz are recounted in this meaningful tribute to the man commonly known as Satchmo. (Ages 10 and older)

Turner, Glennette T. *Take a Walk in Their Shoes.* Illustrated by Elton C. Fax. New York: E.P. Dutton, 1989. 176 pages.

This volume contains brief biographical essays about 14 African Americans, including Arthur A. Schomburg, Leontyne Price, Garrett A. Morgan, and Ida B. Wells. Each essay is followed by a short dramatization for children to act out. This unique approach brings these achievers to life and provides young readers with easy access to hard-to-find information. (Ages 8–12)

Yates, Elizabeth. *Amos Fortune: Free Man.* Illustrated by Nora Unwin. New York: Puffin, 1989. 192 pages.

Brought in slavery from Africa, Amos Fortune was first owned by a Quaker and later by a tanner who taught him a trade and allowed him to buy his freedom. (Ages 8–12)

The Arts, Sports, and Entertainment

Bryan, Ashley. *I'm Going to Sing: Black American Spirituals.* Illustrated by Ashley Bryan. New York: Macmillan, Atheneum, 1982. 64 pages.

Block printings illustrate this collection of 25 African-American spirituals, which includes lyrics as well as musical accompaniment. A useful history of spirituals helps children understand the development of this musical genre. (Ages 7 and older)

————. *All Night, All Day: A Child's First Book of African-American Spirituals.* Illustrated by Ashley Bryan. New York: Macmillan, Atheneum, 1991. 48 pages.

This richly illustrated collection offers an excellent introduction to the historic and distinctive music of African-American spirituals. The book includes the lyrics to 20 spirituals along with music for accompaniment. (Ages 3–9)

Golenbock, Peter. *Teammates.* Illustrated by Paul Bacon. San Diego: Harcourt Brace Jovanovich, Gulliver Books, 1990. 32 pages.

This moving account of segregation, racism, and personal courage features the former Negro Leagues, Brooklyn Dodgers General Manager Branch Rickey, first baseman Jackie Robinson, and shortstop Pee Wee Reese. Archival photographs and full-color illustrations recount the integration of professional baseball and the 1947 season of Jackie Robinson, the first African-American player in the modern major leagues. (Ages 5–10)

Haldane, Suzanne. *Painting Faces.* New York: E.P. Dutton, 1988. 32 pages.

Full-color photographs and a straightforward narrative provide readers with an introduction to the history and art of face painting. Various groups who practice face painting are described, including the Southeast Nuba people of the Sudan; Native Americans in North and Central America; opera and theater performers in India, China, and Japan; and clowns. Complete directions for face painting and a list of needed supplies are included. (Ages 5–12)

Haskins, James. *Black Music in America: A History through Its People.* New York: Harper & Row, T.Y. Crowell, 1987. 224 pages.

The author traces the history of black music in America from the music of enslaved people brought in chains from Africa to the music of such contemporary artists as Michael Jackson, Quincy Jones, and Wynton Marsalis. The book features sections on ragtime, blues, jazz, black Renaissance, opera, and soul. (Ages 12 and older)

———. *Black Dance in America.* New York: HarperCollins, T.Y. Crowell, 1990. 240 pages.

The history of African-American dance comes to life with photographs and a lively narrative. Special attention is given to the important artists who influenced black dance in the United States. (Ages 12 and older)

———. *Black Theater in America.* New York: HarperCollins, 1991. 160 pages.

The achievements of African Americans in the theater from the early 1800s to the present are chronicled in this valuable book. (Ages 12 and older)

Langstaff, John, ed. *Climbing Jacob's Ladder: Heroes of the Bible in African-American Spirituals.* Illustrated by Ashley Bryan. New York: Macmillan, McElderry, 1991. 32 pages.

This carefully illustrated collection of African-American spirituals highlights nine heroes of the Old Testament. The book features background information as well as piano accompaniments and guitar chords. (All ages)

Mattox, Cheryl W. *Shake It to the One That You Love the Best: Play Songs and Lullabies from Black Musical Traditions.* (book/cassette set) Illustrated by Varnette P. Honeywood and Brenda Joysmith. El Sobrante, Calif.: Warren-Mattox Productions, 1990.

This beautifully designed collection contains the music and lyrics for 16 play songs and 10 lullabies. Strips of Kente cloth border each entry, and paintings by gallery artists Varnette P. Honeywood and Brenda Joysmith provide a perfect complement to the spirit of the songs. (All ages)

Mayers, Florence C. *ABC: Egyptian Art from the Brooklyn Museum.* New York: Abrams, 1988. 32 pages.

The photographs in this book, which is part of a series that uses the collections of various museums to illustrate the ABCs for children, detail museum objects from ancient Egypt. Each of the photographs is briefly explained and carefully documented. (Ages 3 and older)

Price, Leontyne. *Aïda.* Illustrated by Leo and Diane Dillon. San Diego: Harcourt Brace Jovanovich, Gulliver Books, 1990. 32 pages.

Opera star Leontyne Price retells *Aïda's* narrative in this richly illustrated volume based on the opera by Guiseppe Verdi. In a storyteller's note at the end of the book, Price describes the qualities she most admires in the Ethiopian princess, including her nobility, strength, and courage, as well as her love for her country and its people. These qualities are vividly expressed in the illustrators' dramatic costuming, inventive staging, and effective use of ancient Egyptian images. (Ages 7–14)

Schmidt, Diane. *I Am a Jesse White Tumbler.* Morton Grove, Ill.: Whitman, 1990. 40 pages.

In this photodocumentary, Kenyon Conner, who has been a member of the famous Jesse White tumbling team since he was five years old, describes the far-reaching effects the team has had on his life and the lives of others. The book's photographs, which show the Chicago-based team performing, clearly illustrate the combination of personal discipline, tumbling expertise, team cooperation, and stage presence required of all Jesse White tumblers. (Ages 7–12)

Strickland, Dorothy S., ed. *Listen Children: An Anthology of Black Literature.* With a foreword by Coretta Scott King. Illustrated by Leo and Diane Dillon. New York: Bantam, Starfire, 1986. 176 pages.

This collection of short works by African-American writers is a celebration of black pride and the joys of youth. Among the authors represented are Lucille Clifton, Langston Hughes, Wilma Rudolph, and Alice Childress. Original sources are cited so that interested readers may pursue an author's work further. (Ages 7 and older)

Sullivan, Charles, ed. *Children of Promise: African-American Literature and Art for Young People.* New York: Abrams, 1991. 128 pages.

More than 100 readings, poems, and songs as well as reproductions of photographs, paintings, and sculpture are included in this excellent anthology focusing on works by and about African Americans. Frederick Douglass, Phillis Wheatley, Gwendolyn Brooks, Langston Hughes, Martin Luther King, Jr., Jacob Lawrence, Henry O. Tanner, and Romare Bearden are only a few of the many notable writers and artists represented. (Ages 10 and older)

Walker, David A., and James Haskins. *Double Dutch.* Hillside, N.J.: Enslow Publishers, 1986. 64 pages.

This fascinating book offers a brief history of the organized team sport of Double Dutch rope jumping and provides detailed instructions for basic and advanced techniques. Black-and-white photographs and drawings illustrate various aspects of this popular and fast-growing sport. (Ages 7–14)

Seasons and Celebrations

Chocolate, Deborah M. Newton. *Kwanzaa.* Illustrated by Melodye Rosales. Chicago: Childrens Press, 1990. 32 pages.

This first-person narrative describes the contemporary seven-day African-American holiday that celebrates kinship, gathering, and African heritage. (Ages 4–9)

Clifton, Lucille. *Don't You Remember?* Illustrated by Evaline Ness. New York: E.P. Dutton, 1973. 32 pages.

Until her birthday finally comes, a young girl thinks that everyone makes promises to her that only she remembers. (Ages 5–7)

Haley, Alex. *A Different Kind of Christmas.* New York: Doubleday, 1988. 112 pages.

Set in 1855, this unforgettable adventure tells the story of a young white Southerner who becomes involved in the Underground Railroad and in a slave's Christmas Eve escape attempt. This touching account tells of physical and moral courage. (Ages 12 and older)

Hamilton, Virginia. *The Bells of Christmas.* Illustrated by Lambert Davis. San Diego: Harcourt Brace Jovanovich, 1989. 60 pages.

This book recaptures the Christmas season of 1890 for an African-American family in Ohio. The story tells of 12-year-old Jason Bell, his loving family, and their warm expressions of holiday joy. The carefully researched text and full-color art evoke the way of life of the time period. (Ages 5–11)

Howard, Elizabeth Fitzgerald. *Chita's Christmas Tree.* Illustrated by Floyd Cooper. New York: Macmillan, Bradbury Press, 1989. 32 pages.

Six brief episodes describe a little girl's excitement as she anticipates the coming of Christmas in Baltimore in 1911. The story is based on the early remembrances of Elizabeth McCard, the daughter of one of Baltimore's first African-American physicians. The author, Elizabeth Howard, is McCard's cousin. (Ages 3–6)

Laird, Elizabeth. *The Road to Bethlehem: An Ethiopian Nativity.* With a foreword by Terry Waite. New York: Henry Holt, 1987. 32 pages.

Hundreds of years ago Ethiopian stories about the birth of Jesus were illustrated by royal commission. Reproduced here in vivid colors, the hand-painted manuscripts provide intriguing variations on the Christmas story. (Ages 6 and older)

Langstaff, John, ed. *What a Morning! The Christmas Story in Black Spirituals.* Illustrated by Ashley Bryan. New York: Macmillan, McElderry, 1987. 32 pages.

The Christmas story is told through five African-American spirituals, chronologically arranged in this lavishly illustrated book. Brief Biblical quotations place each of the spirituals within a religious context. Of special interest are Bryan's shining portraits of a black nativity. (Ages 3 and older)

Lowery, Linda. *Martin Luther King Day.* Illustrated by Hetty Mitchell. Minneapolis: Carolrhoda Books, 1987. 56 pages.

This easy-to-read book focuses on Martin Luther King Day, first celebrated nationally in 1986 in observance of King's birthday. Each page is illustrated, many with full-color drawings. (Ages 4–9)

McClester, Cedric. *Kwanzaa: Everything You Always Wanted to Know But Didn't Know Where to Ask.* New York: Gumbs and Thomas, 1985. 36 pages.

Millions of Americans today observe Kwanzaa, the African-American holiday celebrated from December 26 to January 1. The festival reaffirms the rich cultural heritage of African Americans. This book includes recipes, clothing, and home-decorating suggestions as well as a concise history of Kwanzaa, its principles, and its symbols. Black-and-white photographs and drawings illustrate the text. (Ages 5–13)

McKissack, Patricia C. *Our Martin Luther King Book.* Illustrated by Helen Endres. Mankato, Minn.: Child's World, 1986. 32 pages.

This collection of activities will help young children celebrate Martin Luther King Day. Background information about the American civil rights movement and about King's life are included. (Ages 3–7)

Porter, A.P. *Kwanzaa.* Illustrated by Janice Lee Porter. Minneapolis: Carolrhoda Books, 1991. 48 pages.

Illustrated with soft, colored-pencil drawings, this attractive book examines the historical roots of the African-American cultural festival of Kwanzaa. The book discusses the essential *nguzo saba,* the seven principles of Kwanzaa, and introduces the relevant Swahili terms for the symbols of the holiday with simple explanations, clear translations, and a helpful pronunciation guide. (Ages 5–9)

Schotter, Roni. *Efan the Great.* Illustrated by Rodney Pate. New York: Lothrop, Lee & Shepard, 1986. 32 pages.

In this delightful book, a young boy works to buy a Christmas tree for his neighborhood. (Ages 7–10)

Steptoe, John. *Birthday.* Illustrated by John Steptoe. New York: Henry Holt, 1991. 32 pages.

The people of an imaginary African community help Javaka celebrate his eighth birthday in this richly illustrated picture book. (Ages 3–8)

Walter, Mildred Pitts. *Have a Happy . . .* Illustrated by Carole Byard. New York: Avon, Camelot, 1990. 96 pages.

Celebrating Kwanzaa, Christmas, birthdays, and New Year's is difficult for 11-year-old Chris because his father is unemployed. By creating handmade gifts, Chris achieves a better understanding of the meaning of Kwanzaa. This easy-to-read novel is characterized by realistic interactions among family members. Also included are full-page black-and-white illustrations, information about Kwanzaa, and a Swahili glossary. (Ages 5–12)

Other Places

Berry, James. *A Thief in the Village and Other Stories of Jamaica.* New York: Puffin, 1990. 156 pages.

Nine short stories of childhood reflect everyday life on the island of Jamaica. (Ages 9 and older)

Chiasson, John. *African Journey.* New York: Macmillan, Bradbury Press, 1987. 64 pages.

Short photo essays depict life in six very different African locations and demonstrate how nature affects living conditions. (Ages 9–11)

Daly, Niki. *Not So Fast, Songololo.* New York: Puffin, 1987. 32 pages.

Malusi, a black South African child, is criticized for always lagging behind. When Malusi accompanies his grandmother on a shopping trip, he finds that he moves at just the right speed for his slow-walking grandma. Full-color watercolor paintings enhance the story of this loving relationship between a child and grandparent. (Ages 3–7)

Feelings, Muriel. *Jambo Means Hello: Swahili Alphabet Book.* Illustrated by Tom Feelings. New York: Dial Books, 1985. 56 pages.

The sights and sounds of Africa come to life as children learn the Swahili alphabet in this richly illustrated picture book. (Ages 5–8)

———. *Moja Means One: Swahili Counting Book.* Illustrated by Tom Feelings. New York: Dial Books, 1987. 32 pages.

Outstanding lithographs of East African people illustrate this fascinating book, which teaches children to count in the Swahili language. (Ages 3–8)

Gordon, Sheila. *Waiting for the Rain: A Novel of South Africa.* New York: Bantam, Starfire, 1989. 224 pages.

In this gripping account, two children—a white boy named Frikkie and a black boy named Tengo—become friends during Frikkie's visits to his uncle's farm in the South African veld. Frikkie increasingly dislikes school. Tengo, however, yearns for an education and hates his family's subjugated place in society. When Frikkie and Tengo meet years later as soldier and student, a tense and startling interracial conflict results. (Ages 12 and older)

Gray, Nigel. *A Country Far Away.* Illustrated by Philippe Dupasquier. New York: Orchard, 1991. 32 pages.

A simple, first-person narrative and two sets of compelling illustrations combine to effectively describe the parallel lives of two children, one an African boy who lives in a rural village and the other a Western boy who lives in a city. (Ages 5–6)

Greenfield, Eloise. *Africa Dream.* Illustrated by Carole Byard. New York: Harper & Row, T.Y. Crowell, 1989. 32 pages.

Pencil drawings highlight this book-length poem that follows a young girl's fantasy about shopping in a marketplace, riding a donkey, and being welcomed by her granddaddy. (Ages 4–8)

———. *Under the Sunday Tree.* Illustrated by Amos Ferguson. New York: HarperCollins, Trophy, 1991. 48 pages.

Colorful folk art illustrates this collection of 20 poems that celebrate everyday life in the Bahamas from a child's perspective. (Ages 6–11)

Grifalconi, Ann. *The Village of Round and Square Houses.* Illustrated by Ann Grifalconi. Boston: Little, Brown, 1986. 32 pages.

A small, peaceful village in Cameroon is like no other—the men there live in square houses while the women live in round houses. Young Osa learns the story of how this came to be from her wise and loving grandmother, the best storyteller in the village. Rich, bold illustrations complement this book's engaging narrative. (Ages 4–9)

———. *Darkness and the Butterfly.* Illustrated by Ann Grifalconi. Boston: Little, Brown, 1987. 32 pages.

While playing during the day, little Osa is fearless; at night she is afraid of the dark. A visit to the Wise Woman enables Osa to overcome her fear. Strong, vivid images enrich the story. (Ages 5–9)

———. *Osa's Pride.* Illustrated by Ann Grifalconi. Boston: Little, Brown; Joy Street Books, 1990. 32 pages.

The gentle, instructive story her grandmother has sewn into a cloth helps a young girl realize that her stubborn pride is foolish. The book's illustrations capture the beauty of the African village that serves as the setting for the story. (Ages 5–8)

Heide, Florence Parry, and Judith Heide Gilliland. *The Day of Ahmed's Secret.* New York: Lothrop, Lee & Shepard, 1990. 32 pages.

The sights, sounds, and smells of Cairo, Egypt, are captured in this wonderfully illustrated story about a day in the life of Ahmed, a boy who drives a donkey cart through the streets of the city delivering butane gas canisters. At the end of a long day Ahmed tells his family his secret—that he has learned how to write his name. (Ages 5–8)

Joseph, Lynn. *A Wave in Her Pocket: Stories from Trinidad.* Illustrated by Brian Pinkney. New York: Houghton Mifflin, Clarion Books, 1991. 32 pages.

Scratchboard illustrations and the lilting cadences of the West Indies complement the six lively stories that Tantie tells to her grandnieces and grandnephews. The stories introduce readers to many of the exotic characters of Trinidad's rich oral tradition. In a fitting finale, Tantie passes the storytelling torch to one of her grandnieces. (Ages 4–8)

Lessac, Frane. *Caribbean Canvas.* Illustrated by Frane Lessac. New York: Harper & Row, Lippincott, 1989. 24 pages.

A collection of 19 proverbs and poems combined with original paintings of island life create a portrait of Caribbean culture. (Ages 4 and older)

Lewin, Hugh. *Jafta.* Illustrated by Lisa Kopper. Minneapolis: Lerner, First Avenue Editions, 1989. 24 pages.

Soft, rhythmic language and sepia tones enhance this story about Jafta, an African boy whose changing moods and emotions are reflected in his comparisons to the variety of animals around him. (Ages 5–8)

Maartens, Maretha. *Paper Bird: A Novel of South Africa.* New York: Houghton Mifflin, Clarion Books, 1991. 148 pages.

Even though leaving the boundaries of his black South African township brings great danger, 12-year-old Adam, who is responsible for the care of his family, must go to the city to earn money selling newspapers. (Ages 9–12)

Margolies, Barbara A.   *Rehema's Journey: A Visit in Tanzania.*
New York: Scholastic, 1990.   32 pages.

On her first departure from her mountain village home, nine-year-old Rehema accompanies her father to the wildlife park where he works. This handsome photo essay, which includes a glossary of Swahili words, provides readers with roadside glimpses of daily life in Tanzania and reveals Rehema's responses to her adventure.   (Ages 9–12)

Musgrove, Margaret.   *Ashanti to Zulu: African Traditions.*
Illustrated by Leo and Diane Dillon.   New York: Dial Books, 1980.
32 pages.

This collection of vignettes, one for each letter of the alphabet, explores the customs, values, and philosophies of African peoples.   (Ages 5–9)

Naidoo, Beverly.   *Journey to Jo'Burg: A South African Story.*
Illustrated by Eric Velasquez.   New York: Harper & Row, Trophy, 1988.   96 pages.

Faced with the sudden illness of their baby sister, 13-year-old Naledi and her younger brother, Tiro, bravely set out from their village to find their mother, who works as a servant in Johannesburg. When they reach the city, the youngsters see for themselves the brutal effects of apartheid.   (Ages 9–13)

Seed, Jenny.   *Ntombi's Song. Illustrated by Anno Berry.*   Boston:
Beacon, 1989.   48 pages.

This picture book tells the story of a black South African child named Ntombi who proudly goes into town on her own to run an errand for her mother. Ntombi feels very brave until she reaches a forest that she fears is haunted. She bolsters her courage by singing a special song that her mother made up for her when she was born.   (Ages 5–8)

Tadjo, Véronique.   *Lord of the Dance: An African Retelling.*   New
York: Harper & Row, Lippincott, 1989.   32 pages.

A strong, rhythmic beat drives this poem about the Senufo people of Côte d'Ivoire and the sacred masks that they believe represent the spirits. This powerful poem, illustrated in the distinctive style of Senufo art, serves as a valuable introduction to West African art, culture, and music.   (Ages 5–9)

Zaslavsky, Claudia. *Count on Your Fingers African Style.* Illustrated by Jerry Pinkney. New York: Harper & Row, T.Y. Crowell, 1980. 32 pages.

Various traditional methods of West African finger counting are demonstrated within the setting of a modern marketplace. (Ages 5–10)

Folktales and Legends

Aardema, Verna. *Why Mosquitoes Buzz in People's Ears: A West African Tale.* Illustrated by Leo and Diane Dillon. New York: Dial Books, 1978. 32 pages.

Just by telling a tall tale, a mosquito sets off a chain of events that ends with the death of a baby owl. Now, Mother Owl will not call the sun up in the morning. King Lion must find out what happened and punish the mosquito for his foolishness. (Ages 4–8)

———. *Who's in Rabbit's House: A Masai Tale.* Illustrated by Leo and Diane Dillon. New York: Dial Books, 1979. 32 pages.

Superb illustrations help convey the comic spirit of this story, which describes how to get an intruder out of rabbit's house without tearing his house down. A traditional Masai play performed by actors in animal masks is the basis for this lively story. (Ages 5–8)

———. *Bringing the Rain to Kapiti Plain: A Nandi Tale.* Illustrated by Beatrix Vidal. New York: Dial Books, 1983. 32 pages.

This East African folktale is retold using a cumulative refrain. Brilliant colors and stylized forms illustrate the story. (Ages 4–9)

———. *Rabbit Makes a Monkey of Lion: A Swahili Tale.* Illustrated by Jerry Pinkney. New York: Dial Books, 1989. 32 pages.

Rabbit is determined to get the honey in a beehive hanging in Lion's calabash tree. Using Turtle and Bush-rat as helpers, Rabbit outwits the slow-moving Lion. Pinkney's pencil-and-watercolor illustrations are as dramatic from a distance as they are close up, making this lengthy, action-filled tale from Zanzibar a natural choice for group use. (Ages 4–9)

———. *Traveling to Tondo: A Tale of the Nkundo of Zaire.* Illustrated by Will Hillenbrand. New York: Alfred A. Knopf, 1991. 40 pages.

While on a journey to meet his bride-to-be, a foolish civet cat is easily sidetracked by friends. Words in the Lonkundo language and lush art enhance this funny tale from Zaire. (Ages 5–9)

Achebe, Chinua, and John Iroaganachi. *How the Leopard Got His Claws.* With *The Lament of the Deer* by Christopher Okigbo. Illustrated by Per Christiansen. New Rochelle, N.Y.: Third Press, 1973. 32 pages.

When the harmony among the animals of the forest is upset, mild and friendly King Leopard becomes a terror with claws and teeth. (Ages 12 and older)

Bryan, Ashley. *The Cat's Purr.* Illustrated by Ashley Bryan. New York: Macmillan, Atheneum, 1985. 48 pages.

How the cat got its purr is explained in this excellent read-aloud tale from the West Indies. (Ages 4–9)

———. *Lion and the Ostrich Chicks, and Other African Folktales.* Illustrated by Ashley Bryan. New York: Macmillan, Atheneum, 1986. 96 pages.

These four folktales are full of fun, drama, and truth. Told with a smoothly paced rhythm that invites reading aloud, each folktale is carefully illustrated and documented according to its specific cultural source in Africa. (Ages 5–12)

———. *Beat the Story-Drum, Pum-Pum.* Illustrated by Ashley Bryan. New York: Macmillan, Atheneum, 1987. 80 pages.

This collection of five Nigerian folktales offers a humorous and forceful look at several human dilemmas. Colorful illustrations complement these entertaining stories. (Ages 5–12)

———. *The Dancing Granny.* Illustrated by Ashley Bryan. New York: Macmillan, Aladdin, 1987. 64 pages.

Granny outwits the trickster spider Anansi and protects her garden in this spirited West Indian folktale. (Ages 5–9)

————. *Turtle Knows Your Name.* Illustrated by Ashley Bryan. New York: Macmillan, Atheneum, 1989. 32 pages.

Upsilimana Tumpalerado and his grandmother celebrate when the young boy finally learns to say his long name. Turtle overhears the name and helps the boy later. Rhyming phrases and memorable images highlight this West Indian tale. (Ages 3–9)

De Sauza, James. *Brother Anansi and the Cattle Ranch.* Illustrated by Stephen Von Mason. Adapted by Harriet Rohmer. Translated by Rosalma Zubizarreta. San Francisco: Childrens Book Press, 1989. 32 pages.

The wise and lovable trickster spider Anansi discovers that Brother Tiger has won the lottery. Brother Anansi convinces Brother Tiger to buy livestock for a cattle ranch that the two will manage together. This traditional West African folktale, presented in both English and Spanish, is richly illustrated. (Ages 5–9)

Guy, Rosa. *Mother Crocodile: An Uncle Amadou Tale from Senegal.* Illustrated by John Steptoe. New York: Delacorte, 1982. 32 pages.

In this Ovolof tale from Senegal, Mother Crocodile warns her children to swim away. Instead, they close their ears. Only later, when it is almost too late, do they realize the truth in her words. (Ages 4–8)

Hale, Sarah J. *Mary Had a Little Lamb.* Illustrated by Bruce McMillan. New York: Scholastic, 1990. 32 pages.

Clearly reproduced full-color photographs, which show Mary as a contemporary African-American child living in a rural area, give a modern interpretation to this familiar nursery rhyme. An afterword provides a history of the rhyme, the full text of the original 1830 version, and a sample lesson from an 1857 McGuffey Reader that used the rhyme to teach reading. (Ages 3–7)

Haley, Gail E. *A Story, a Story: An African Tale.* Illustrated by Gail E. Haley. New York: Macmillan, Aladdin, 1988. 36 pages.

This handsome picture book, illustrated with brilliant woodcuts, explains how the Anansi stories came to earth. (Ages 6 and older)

Hamilton, Virginia. *The People Could Fly: American Black Folktales.* Illustrated by Leo and Diane Dillon. New York: Alfred A. Knopf, 1985. 192 pages.

Selected especially for children, this anthology of African-American folklore includes 24 finely crafted tales for families to share and people of all ages and backgrounds to enjoy. The use of black English from several cultures, historical notes, and stylized black-and-white illustrations enrich this unique work. (Ages 3 and older)

Harris, Joel C. *Jump on Over! The Adventures of Brer Rabbit and His Family.* Adapted by Van Dyke Parks. Illustrated by Barry Moser. San Diego: Harcourt Brace Jovanovich, 1989. 48 pages.

Told by slaves and first published in 1880, these five stories, which relate how Brer Rabbit outwits Brer Fox, Brer Wolf, and Brer Bear during a drought, are part of an important piece of American folk culture in which brute strength does not triumph. An illustrator's note provides a historical context for the stories. (Ages 5–11)

Hooks, William H. *The Ballad of Belle Dorcas.* Illustrated by Brian Pinkney. New York: Alfred A. Knopf, 1990. 48 pages.

Based on traditional Gullah folklore, this story, which exposes the injustice and cruelty of slavery, tells how beautiful Belle, a free woman, chooses to marry an enslaved man rather than remain free. When Belle's beloved husband is about to be sold, she goes to a conjure woman for a spell to keep him with her. The results of the spell, however, are not what Belle expected. (Ages 7–12)

Hughes, Langston, and Arna Bontemps, eds. *The Book of Negro Folklore.* New York: Dodd, Mead, 1983. 656 pages.

This valuable compendium of black folklore can be used by both teachers and students. (All ages)

Jaquith, Priscilla. *Bo Rabbit Smart for True: Folktales from the Gullah.* Illustrated by Ed Young. New York: Putnam, Philomel, 1981. 55 pages.

Cartoon-like frames border each panel of four trickster tales, which originated in the traditional folklore of the coastal islands of Georgia and South Carolina. The tales are written in the Gullah dialect. Source notes, a brief description of Gullah culture, and a bibliography add to the value of this unusual and highly entertaining book.   (Ages 4–9)

Korty, Carol.   *Plays from African Folktales: With Ideas for Acting, Dance, Costumes, and Music.*   Illustrated by Sandra Cain.   New York: Charles Scribner's, 1975.   128 pages.

This collection includes four plays, all of which are easy to stage and adaptable to a variety of situations. The book also highlights ideas for acting, dance, costumes, and music.   (Ages 8–12)

Lester, Julius.   *The Tales of Uncle Remus: The Adventures of Brer Rabbit.*   Illustrated by Jerry Pinkney.   New York: Dial Books, 1987. 160 pages.

These imaginative retellings of 48 Brer Rabbit stories, written in contemporary black English, give children a new view of Uncle Remus. Pinkney's black-and-white drawings and watercolors complement the lively tales.   (Ages 6–11)

————.   *More Tales of Uncle Remus: Further Adventures of Brer Rabbit, His Friends, Enemies and Others.*   Illustrated by Jerry Pinkney.   New York: Dial Books, 1988.   160 pages.

This companion volume to *The Tales of Uncle Remus: The Adventures of Brer Rabbit* (1987) includes 37 additional stories for children.   (Ages 4 and older)

————.   *How Many Spots Does a Leopard Have? And Other Tales.* Illustrated by David Shannon.   New York: Scholastic, 1989. 80 pages.

African and Jewish stories make up this delightful collection of 12 witty and humorous tales about animals and people who outsmart bigger, tougher, and more powerful opponents in order to teach them a lesson.   (Ages 10–12)

————.   *Black Folktales.*   Illustrated by Tom Feelings.   New York: Grove Weidenfeld, 1991.   160 pages.

The author brings a fresh, vibrant approach to the timeless truths presented in this collection of African and African-American folktales.   (Ages 12 and older)

Lester, Julius, and Phyllis J. Fogelman. *Further Tales of Uncle Remus: The Misadventures of Brer Rabbit, Brer Fox, Brer Wolf, the Doodang, and All the Other Creatures.* Illustrated by Jerry Pinkney. New York: Dial Books, 1990. 160 pages.

Lester's third collection of Uncle Remus stories includes more than 30 tales about Brer Rabbit, Miz Cricket, and Brer Turtle— including the favorite "Tailypo!" Crisp, fresh illustrations enhance the timeless quality of the stories. (All ages)

Michels, Barbara, and Bettye White, eds. *Apples on a Stick: The Folklore of Black Children.* Illustrated by Jerry Pinkney. New York: Coward-McCann, 1983. 52 pages.

This book of playground rhymes, collected from African-American school children in Houston, Texas, includes hand-clap games, counting and jump-rope rhymes, and nonsense verses. Each page is illustrated with black-and-white pencil drawings that capture the vitality of children at play. (Ages 7–12)

Mollel, Tololwa M. *The Orphan Boy.* Illustrated by Paul Morin. New York: Ticknor & Fields, 1991. 32 pages.

Textured paintings highlight this spectacular rendition of an ancient Masai legend about the planet Venus and the extraordinary boy who comes to live with a lonely old man until a trust is broken. (Ages 6–8)

Robinson, Dorothy W. *The Legend of Africania.* Illustrated by Herbert Temple. Chicago: Johnson Publishing, 1974. 32 pages.

This allegorical tale tells of Africa's struggle against attacks on its people and its land. (Ages 5–10)

San Souci, Robert D. *The Boy and the Ghost.* Illustrated by Brian Pinkney. New York: Simon & Schuster, 1989. 32 pages.

In this African-American tale, a young boy named Thomas—the middle child in a large family—sets out to earn some money, taking with him a few supplies and a lot of advice. After showing kindness to a stranger, Thomas wins a treasure for his family by staying all night in a haunted house. The story's fast pace and large, effective illustrations make it a good choice for group use. (Ages 5–9)

————. *The Talking Eggs.* Illustrated by Jerry Pinkney. New York: Dial Books, 1989. 32 pages.

This Creole folktale features two sisters—Rose, who is spoiled and lazy, and Blanche, who is kind and hardworking. A mysterious woman in the woods gives the girls identical tasks, and Blanche is rewarded for her trust and obedience. This beautiful story features characters brilliantly illustrated by Pinkney's drawings and paintings. (Ages 4–9)

Steptoe, John. *Mufaro's Beautiful Daughters: An African Tale.* Illustrated by John Steptoe. New York: Lothrop, Lee & Shepard, 1987. 32 pages.

Two beautiful sisters—one vain, the other kind—compete for the king's attention when he announces that he is looking for a wife. Steptoe's pen-and-ink watercolors skillfully detail the natural beauty of Zimbabwe. (Ages 4–8)

Swann, Brian. *A Basket Full of White Eggs: Riddle-Poems.* Illustrated by Ponder Goembel. New York: Orchard, 1988. 32 pages.

Fifteen challenging riddles from different cultures, including the Yoruba, are arranged in a morning-to-night cycle. Readers can find subtle clues for each riddle in the full-color illustrations. All sources are fully documented. (Ages 5–9)

Walter, Mildred Pitts. *Brother to the Wind.* Illustrated by Leo and Diane Dillon. New York: Lothrop, Lee & Shepard, 1985. 32 pages.

The author draws on the symbols found in traditional African tales to create an imaginative story about a boy who asks Good Snake to help him learn to fly. Full-color illustrations enhance the creative themes of the text. (Ages 5–9)

Indexes

Index of Authors and Illustrators

A

A.B.C. Task Force Staff, 58
Aardema, Verna, 112, 113
Achebe, Chinua, 113
Adler, David A., 91
Adoff, Arnold, 66
Ahlberg, Allan, 66
Ahlberg, Janet, 66
Ajayi, J.F. Ade, 2
Aldred, Lisa, 91
Alexander, Adele Logan, 21
Allen, Robert L., 27
Altman, Susan, 91
Anderson, James D., 7
Andrews, William L., 40
Angelou, Maya, 34
Anti-Defamation League of
    B'nai B'rith, 57
Aptheker, Herbert, 7, 9, 15
Arnold, Thomas St. John, 28
Asante, Molefi K., 7, 45
Ashe, Arthur R., 40
Ashkinaze, Carole, 48
Aten, Jerry, 57
Audette, Anna Held, 74

B

Bacon, Paul, 102
Bailey, Pearl, 66
Baker, Gwendolyn, 52
Baker, Houston A., Jr., 35
Baldwin, James, 45
Banks, Cherry A. McGee, 52
Banks, James A., 52
Baptiste, H. Prentice, Jr., 53, 57
Baptiste, Mira L., 57
Barker, Lucius J., 46
Barlow, William, 41
Barnes, Marian E., 42
Barnett, Moneta, 72
Baruth, Leroy G., 53
Bearden, Romare, 77

Bell, Bernard W., 40
Bell, Derrick, 46
Bell, Malcolm, 15
Bennett, Christine I., 53
Bennett, Lerone, 8
Benson, Kathleen, 95
Bentley, Judith, 91
Berleth, Richard, 84
Berlin, Ira, 15, 22
Bernal, Martin, 2
Berry, Anno, 111
Berry, James, 107
Berry, Mary Frances, 8
Bethel, Elizabeth R., 22
Billingsley, Andrew, 8
Binch, Caroline, 73, 74
Blackett, R.J.M., 34
Blassingame, John W., 8, 15
Blassingame, Wyatt, 92
Blauner, Bob, 46
Blight, David W., 35
Blockson, Charles L., 16
Blue, Rose, 92
Blume, Judy, 66
Bogart, Jo Ellen, 67
Bogle, Donald, 40
Bohannan, Paul, 2
Bond, Horace Mann, 8
Bond, Sandra Turner, 72
Bontemps, Arna, 115
Boyd, Candy Dawson, 67
Boyer, James, 53
Boyette, Michael, 46
Boyette, Randi, 46
Bracey, John H., Jr., 32
Branch, Taylor, 30
Brandt, Nat, 16
Broderick, Dorothy M., 57
Brooks, Gwendolyn, 67
Brotz, Howard, 8
Brown, Sterling A., 41
Brown, Thomas J., 57
Bryan, Ashley, 101, 103, 106,
    113, 114

Byard, Carole, 78, 84, 107,
    109

C

Cabell, Edward J., 14
Cain, Sandra, 116
Caines, Jeannette, 68
Campbell, Edward D.C., Jr., 16
Cantor, George, 9
Carlstrom, Nancy W., 68
Carroll, John M., 35
Carson, Clayborne, 30, 31
Carter, Stephen L., 46
Carty, Leo, 77
Casilla, Robert, 75, 91
Celsi, Teresa, 92
Cheatham, Harold E., 46
Chiasson, John, 108
Childers, Norman, 87
Childress, Alice, 68
Chinn, Philip C., 54
Chocolate, Deborah M.
    Newton, 105
Christiansen, Per, 113
Clark, Reginald M., 53
Clift, Virgil A., 12
Clifton, Lucille, 69, 105
Cohen, William, 25
Collier, James L., 92
Comer, James P., 28
Cook, Mercer, 3
Cooper, Floyd, 72, 105
Cooper, Wayne F., 35
Cooperative Children's Book
    Center, 58
Cornish, Dudley T., 23
Cortner, Richard C., 28
Cox, LaWanda, 23
Cox, Thomas C., 26
Creel, Margaret W., 16
Cross, William E., Jr., 47
Crowder, Michael, 2
Cummings, Pat, 68, 81, 82, 83

Curry, Leonard P., 21
Curtin, Philip D., 2
Curtis, Gavin, 69
Cwiklik, Robert, 92

D

Daly, Niki, 108
Daniel, Pete, 28
Dates, Jannette L., 41
Davidson, Basil, 2, 3
Davidson, Ellen, 61
Davis, Arthur P., 41
Davis, Burke, 92
Davis, David B., 16
Davis, Lambert, 105
Davis, Ossie, 93
Deeter, Catherine, 82
De Graft-Johnson, J.C., 3
De Jager, Marjolijn, 3
Della Piana, Leandro, 98
Derman-Sparks, Louise, 58
De Sauza, James, 114
De Veaux, Alexis, 70, 93
De Vries, James E., 26
DiGrazia, Thomas, 69
Dillon, Diane, 71, 77, 103, 104, 111, 112, 115, 118
Dillon, Leo, 71, 77, 103, 104, 111, 112, 115, 118
Diop, Cheikh Anta, 3
Domhoff, William G., 49
Dorsey-Gaines, Catherine, 56
Douglass, Frederick, 35
Drago, Edmund L., 23
Dragonwagon, Crescent, 70
Drake, St. Clair, 3
Duberman, Martin B., 35
Du Bois, W.E.B., 4, 9, 23, 26
Duckett, Alfred, 99
Dupasquier, Philippe, 108
Duster, Alfreda M., 40

E

Edsall, Mary D., 47
Edsall, Thomas B., 47
Eldridge, Richard, 37
Ely, Melvin P., 41
Endres, Helen, 106
Evans, Mari, 41

F

Fabre, Michel, 42
Fax, Elton C., 93, 101
Fayer, Steve, 31
Feelings, Muriel, 108
Feelings, Tom, 71, 73, 85, 86, 108, 116
Feinberg, Brian, 93
Ferguson, Amos, 109
Ferguson, Leland, 17
Ferris, Jeri, 93
Ferris, William, 14
Fields, Julia, 70
Fine, Sidney, 28
Fisher, Leonard Everett, 87
Fleischman, Paul, 85
Florian, Douglas, 70
Flournoy, Valerie, 71
Fogelman, Phyllis J., 117
Foner, Eric, 23
Foner, Philip S., 9, 21
Forbes, Jack, 9
Ford, Bernette G., 75
Ford, George, 71, 72, 75, 97
Forman, James, 31
Fox-Genovese, Elizabeth, 17
Franklin, John Hope, 9, 35
Frederickson, George M., 10
Freedman, Russell, 85
Froschl, Merle, 58
Fuchs, Bernie, 100

G

Gaillard, Frye, 47
Garcia, Ricardo L., 54
Garrow, David J., 36
Gates, Henry L., Jr., 36, 43
Gatewood, Willard, 26
Giddings, Paula, 10
Gilchrist, Jan Spivey, 72, 86
Gilliland, Judith Heide, 110
Gilman, Michael, 94
Ginsburg, Max, 89, 90
Giovanni, Nikki, 71
Glatthaar, Joseph T., 24
Goembel, Ponder, 118
Goldfield, David R., 47
Goldman, Peter L., 36
Golenbock, Peter, 102
Gollnick, Donna M., 54
Gordon, Sheila, 108
Goss, Linda, 42
Graham, Hugh D., 31
Grant, Carl A., 54, 56, 58
Gray, Nigel, 108
Greene, Lorenzo J., 36
Greenfield, Eloise, 71, 72, 109
Grifalconi, Ann, 69, 109
Grimes, Nikki, 73
Gutman, Herbert G., 17
Guy, Rosa, 73, 114

H

Haber, Louis, 94
Haldane, Suzanne, 102
Hale, Sarah J., 114
Hale-Benson, Janice E., 54
Haley, Alex, 37, 105
Haley, Gail E., 114
Hamilton, Charles V., 36
Hamilton, Kenneth Marvin, 26
Hamilton, Virginia, 73, 74, 85, 86, 94, 105, 115
Hampton, Henry, 31

Index of Authors and Illustrators

Hancock, Sibyl, 94
Handlin, Sean, 56
Hanna, Cheryl, 70
Hansen, Joyce, 74
Hanson, Peter E., 93
Harding, Vincent, 17
Harlan, Louis, 36
Harris, Joel C., 115
Harris, Joseph E., 4
Harris, William, 29
Hartigan, Lynda Roscoe, 42
Haskins, James, 94, 95, 102, 104
Hatch, Roger D., 47
Hay, Margaret Jean, 4
Haynes, Jerry, 94
Hays, Michael, 90
Hedgepeth, Chester M., Jr., 42
Heide, Florence Parry, 110
Hermann, Janet S., 24
Hernandez, Hilda, 54
Hillenbrand, Will, 113
Hine, Darlene C., 10
Hoffman, Mary, 74
Hoffman, Ronald, 15
Honeywood, Varnette P., 103
Hooks, William H., 115
Hoose, Phillip M., 42
Hopkins, Lee B., 74
Hopson, Derek S., 49
Horning, Kathleen T., 58
Hornsby, Alton, Jr., 10
Horton, James O., 21
Horton, Lois E., 21
Howard, Elizabeth Fitzgerald, 75, 105
Hudson, Cheryl W., 75
Hudson, Wade, 75, 95
Hughes, Langston, 10, 42, 76, 115
Hull, Richard W., 4
Humphrey, Kathryn L., 96
Hunter, Kristin, 76
Hurston, Zora Neale, 37

I

Igus, Toyomi, 96
International Scientific Committee for the Drafting of a General History of Africa, 4
Ione, Carole, 11
Iroaganachi, John, 113

J

Jackson, Jesse L., 47
Jackson, John G., 5
James, Howard, 17
James, Portia, 11
Jaquith, Priscilla, 115
Jaynes, Gerald D., 47
Jencks, Christopher, 48
Johnson, Angela, 76
Johnson, Dianne, 59
Johnson, Dolores, 84
Johnson, Herschel, 77
Johnson, Michael P., 22
Jonas, Ann, 77
Jones, Jacqueline, 11
Jones-Jackson, Patricia, 11
Jordan, Winthrop D., 18
Joseph, Lynn, 110
Joyce, Joyce Ann, 41
Joyner, Charles, 18
Joysmith, Brenda, 103

K

Kaminski, John P., 18
Katz, William L., 11, 86, 96
Kaufman, Jonathan, 48
Keith, Eros, 85
Kellner, Bruce, 43
Kemble, Frances Anne, 18
Kendall, Frances E., 59
Kerman, Cynthia E., 37
King, Edith W., 59

King, Martin Luther, Jr., 32
Klots, Steve, 96
Kluger, Richard, 32
Knight, Franklin W., 5
Kopper, Lisa, 110
Korty, Carol, 116
Kozol, Jonathan, 48
Kruse, Ginny Moore, 58
Kulikoff, Allan, 18
Kunene, Mazisi, 5

L

Laird, Elizabeth, 106
Langstaff, John, 103, 106
Larsen, Rebecca, 96
Lay, Shawn, 29
Lee, Ulysses, 41
Leffler, Richard, 18
Leigh, Wilhelmina, 48
Lemann, Nicholas, 29
Lessac, Frane, 110
Lester, Julius, 86, 116, 117
Lewin, Hugh, 110
Lewis, Ronald L., 9
Lincoln, C. Eric, 12
Lindgren, Merri V., 58
Linnemann, Russell, 37
Little, Lessie Jones, 86
Littlefield, Daniel C., 18
Litwack, Leon F., 24, 37
Lockhart, David, 89
Logan, Rayford W., 12
Long, Richard A., 24, 43
Loveland, Anne C., 37
Low, Augustus W., 12
Lowery, Linda, 106
Luker, Ralph E., 31
Lynch, James, 52
Lyons, Mary E., 96

M

Maartens, Maretha, 110
MacCann, Donnarae, 59, 60

Major, Geri, 12
Malcolm X, 37
Malson, Micheline, 12
Mamiya, Lawrence H., 12
Manning, Kenneth R., 38
Manning, M. Lee, 53
Marable, Manning, 48
Margolies, Barbara A., 111
Marie, D., 87
Martin Luther King, Jr., Center for Nonviolent Social Change, 60
Martins, George, 71
Mathis, Sharon Bell, 77, 78, 97
Mattox, Cheryl W., 103
Mattson, Mark T., 7
Mayers, Florence C., 103
McAdam, Doug, 32
McClester, Cedric, 106
McDaniel, George W., 26
McElroy, Guy C., 43
McFeely, William S., 38
McKissack, Frederick, 78, 87, 97
McKissack, Patricia C., 78, 87, 97, 106
McMillan, Bruce, 114
McMillen, Neil R., 29
McPherson, James M., 24
Meier, August, 29, 32, 35, 37
Mellon, James, 19
Meltzer, Milton, 10, 42, 87, 88
Mendez, Phil, 78
Michels, Barbara, 117
Miller, Keith D., 33
Milton, Joyce, 98
Mitchell, Hetty, 106
Mollel, Tololwa M., 117
Moore, Emily, 78, 79
Moore, Yvette, 88
Morin, Paul, 117
Morris, Aldon D., 33
Moser, Barry, 115
Moss, Alfred A., Jr., 9, 27

Murray, Pauli, 38
Musgrove, Margaret, 111
Myers, Walter Dean, 79, 88

N

Naden, Corinne J., 92
Naidoo, Beverly, 111
Nalty, Bernard C., 12
Narahashi, Keiko, 80
Nash, Gary B., 19
National Association of State Boards of Education, 54
National Council for the Social Studies, 55
Ness, Evaline, 105
Neverdon-Morton, Cynthia, 27
New York Public Library, 60
Nieto, Sonia, 55

O

Oates, Stephen B., 38
O'Dell, Scott, 88
Orfield, Gary, 48
Orlov, Ann, 56
Owens, Leslie Howard, 19

P

Page, James A., 43
Pakenham, Thomas, 5
Palmer, Colin A., 5
Pate, Rodney, 79, 107
Patterson, Charles, 98
Patterson, Lillie, 98
Pease, Jane H., 19, 24
Pease, William H., 19, 24
Pelz, Ruth, 98
Peterson, Paul E., 48
Peterson, Robert, 43
Petry, Ann, 98
Pfeffer, Paula F., 38

Phinney, Jean S., 55
Piersen, William D., 22
Pinkney, Brian, 110, 115, 117
Pinkney, Jerry, 68, 70, 71, 78, 89, 112, 116, 117, 118
Ploski, Harry A., 13
Poitier, Sidney, 99
Ponce, Wallace Y., 14
Porter, A.P., 107
Porter, Janice Lee, 107
Portland Public Schools, 60
Powell-Hopson, Darlene, 49
Preston, Kitty, 99
Price, Leontyne, 103
Proudfoot, Merrill, 33
Putney, Martha S., 22

Q

Quarles, Benjamin, 13

R

Rabinowitz, Howard N., 25
Rachleff, Peter J., 27
Rampersad, Arnold, 38
Ramsey, Patricia G., 60
Ransome, James, 75, 76
Redding, J. Saunders, 41
Revis, Alesia, 72
Reynolds, Barbara, 99
Rice, Kym S., 16
Richard-Amato, Patricia A., 55
Ringgold, Faith, 80
Roark, James L., 22
Roberts, John W., 44
Roberts, Naurice, 99
Robinson, Armstead L., 33
Robinson, Dorothy W., 117
Robinson, Jackie, 99
Rodney, Walter, 5
Rollins, Charlemae H., 100
Rollock, Barbara, 61
Romer, John, 6

Rosales, Melodye, 105
Rose, Phyllis, 39
Rotheram, Mary J., 55
Rozelle, Robert V., 44
Rudwick, Elliott, 29, 32
Russell, Penny A., 31

S

Salemson, Harold J., 3
Sanders, Leslie C., 44
San Souci, Robert D., 117, 118
Schall, Keith L., 29
Scheader, Catherine, 100
Schmidt, Diane, 104
Schniedewind, Nancy, 61
Schotter, Roni, 107
Schroeder, Alan, 100
Schwinger, Loren, 39
Scott, John A., 18
Seed, Jenny, 111
Serfozo, Mary, 80
Seward, James, 100
Sewell, Helen, 76
Shade, Barbara J., 55, 56
Shannon, David, 116
Shapiro, Herbert, 13
Shelby, Anne, 80
Shumate, Jane, 100
Simonsen, Thordis, 39
Sleeter, Christine E., 54, 56, 58
Smith, Edward D., 13
Smith, Kathie B., 100
Snow, Marguerite Ann, 55
Snowden, Frank, 6
Sobel, Mechal, 20
Solbert, Ronni, 67
Soman, David, 76
Southern, Eileen, 44
Springer, Nancy, 80
Sprung, Barbara, 58
Stanley, Diane, 100
Steptoe, John, 66, 80, 107, 114, 118

Sterling, Dorothy, 13
Sterne, Emma G., 89
Stewart, James B., 46, 48
Stewart, Paul W., 14
Stichter, Sharon, 4
Stock, Catherine, 82
Stolz, Mary, 81
Strickland, Dorothy S., 104
Stuckey, Sterling, 20
Suggs, Henry L., 39
Sullivan, Charles, 104
Sullivan, Patricia, 33
Swann, Brian, 118
Swift, David E., 20

T

Tadjo, Véronique, 111
Tanenhaus, Sam, 101
Tate, Eleanora E., 81
Taulbert, Clifton L., 30
Taylor, Denny, 56
Taylor, Mildred D., 89, 90
Temple, Herbert, 117
Terry, Wallace, 33
Thernstrom, Stephen, 56
Thomas, Joyce Carol, 81, 82
Tiedt, Iris M., 61
Tiedt, Pamela L., 61
Trotter, Joe William, Jr., 30
Tucker, Mark, 39
Turkle, Brinton, 69
Turner, Glennette T., 101
Turner, Nat, 20
Turner, William H., 14
Tushnet, Mark V., 34

U

Unwin, Nora, 101

V

Van Sertima, Ivan, 6, 14, 39
Velasquez, Eric, 111

Vennema, Peter, 100
Vercoutter, Jean, 44
Vestal, Herman, 92
Vidal, Beatrix, 112
Von Mason, Stephen, 114

W

Walker, Alice, 82
Walker, Clarence E., 25
Walker, David, 20
Walker, David A., 104
Walker, George F., 21
Walker, Juliet E., 39
Wallerstein, Immanuel, 6
Walter, Mildred Pitts, 82, 83, 107, 118
Walters, Ronald W., 46
Ward, John, 80
Wardlaw, Alvia J., 44
Washburn, Patrick S., 30
Washington, Booker T., 40
Watkins, Frank E., 47
Watling, James, 84
Wayne, Michael, 25
Weisbrot, Robert, 34
Wells, Ida B., 40
Wesley, Charles H., 14
Wesley, Valerie W., 95
White, Bettye, 117
Wilkinson, Brenda, 83
Williams, Chancellor, 7
Williams, James, 13
Williams, Juan, 34
Williams, Robin M., Jr., 47
Williams, Vera B., 83
Willis-Thomas, Deborah, 45
Wilson, Beth P., 84
Wilson, Charles R., 14
Wilson, Janet, 67
Wilson, William Julius, 49
Wiltse, Charles, 20
Winston, Michael R., 12
Winter, Jeanette, 90

Woll, Allen, 45
Woodard, Gloria, 59, 60
Woodson, Carter G., 14
Woodson, Jacqueline, 84
Woodward, C. Vann, 27

Y

Yarbrough, Camille, 84
Yates, Elizabeth, 101
Young, Ed, 115

Z

Zangrando, Robert L., 34
Zaslavsky, Claudia, 112
Zweigenhaft, Richard L., 49

Index of Titles

A

A. Philip Randolph: Pioneer of the Civil Rights Movement (Pfeffer), 38

ABC: Egyptian Art from the Brooklyn Museum (Mayers), 103

Adam Clayton Powell, Jr.: The Political Biography of an American Dilemma (Hamilton), 36

Adventures of Amos 'n Andy, The: A Social History of an American Phenomenon (Ely), 41

Affirming Diversity: The Sociopolitical Context of Multicultural Education (Nieto), 55

Africa and Africans (Bohannan and Curtin), 2

Africa and the Modern World (Wallerstein), 6

Africa Dream (Greenfield), 109

African-American Baseline Essays (Portland Public Schools), 60

African-American History (Hughes and Meltzer), 10

African-American Social and Political Thought, 1850–1920 (Brotz), 8

African Cities and Towns before the European Conquest (Hull), 4

African Civilization Revisited: From Antiquity to Modern Times (Davidson), 3

African Genius, The: An Introduction to Social and Cultural History (Davidson), 2

African Glory (De Graft-Johnson), 3

African Journey (Chiasson), 108

African Origin of Civilization, The: Myth or Reality? (Diop), 3

Africans and Their History (Harris), 4

African Slave Trade, The (Davidson), 3

African Women South of the Sahara (Hay and Stichter), 4

Africa Remembered: Narratives by West Africans from the Era of the Slave Trade (Curtin), 2

Afro-American Novel and Its Tradition, The (Bell), 40

Afro-American Women of the South and the Advancement of the Race, 1895–1925 (Neverdon-Morton), 27

Afro-Bets Book of Black Heroes from A to Z: An Introduction to Important Black Achievers for Young Readers (Hudson and Wesley), 95

Afrocentric Idea, The (Asante), 45

After the School Bell Rings (Grant and Sleeter), 54

Aïda (Price), 103

Alain Locke: Reflections on a Modern Renaissance Man (Linnemann), 37

Alesia (Greenfield and Revis), 72

All Night, All Day: A Child's First Book of African-American Spirituals (Bryan), 101

All the Colors of the Race (Adoff), 66

All Times, All Peoples: A World History of Slavery (Meltzer), 87

Amazing Grace (Hoffman), 74

Ambiguous Lives: Free Women of Color in Rural Georgia, 1789–1879 (Alexander), 21

American Negro Academy, The: Voice of the Talented Tenth (Moss), 27

American Negro Slave Revolts (Aptheker), 15

Americans, Too! (Aten), 57

American Tapestry, The: Educating a Nation (National Association of State Boards of Education), 54

Amos Fortune: Free Man (Yates), 101

Ancient Lives: Daily Life in the Egypt of the Pharaohs (Romer), 6

And Still We Rise: Interviews with 50 Black Role Models (Reynolds), 99

And We Are Not Saved: The Elusive Quest for Racial Justice (Bell), 46

Anthony Burns: The Defeat and Triumph of a Fugitive Slave (Hamilton), 94

Anti-Bias Curriculum: Tools for Empowering Young Children (Derman-Sparks and the A.B.C. Task Force Staff), 58

Apples on a Stick: The Folklore of Black Children (Michels and White), 117

Archbishop Tutu of South Africa (Bentley), 91

Aristocrats of Color: The Black Elite, 1880–1920 (Gatewood), 26

Ashanti to Zulu: African Traditions (Musgrove), 111

At Freedom's Edge: Black Mobility and the Southern White Quest for Racial Control, 1861–1915 (Cohen), 25

Aunt Flossie's Hats (and Crab Cakes Later) (Howard), 75

Autobiography of James Thomas, The (Schwinger), 39

Autobiography of Malcolm X, The (Malcolm X), 37

B

Ballad of Belle Dorcas, The (Hooks), 115

Barbara Jordan (Haskins), 94

Basket Full of White Eggs, A: Riddle-Poems (Swann), 118

Battle Cry of Freedom: The Civil War Era (McPherson), 24

Bearing the Cross: Martin Luther King, Jr., and the Southern Christian Leadership Conference (Garrow), 36

Bearing Witness: Selections from African-American Autobiography in the Twentieth Century (Gates), 36

Beat the Story-Drum, Pum-Pum (Bryan), 113

Been in the Storm So Long: The Aftermath of Slavery (Litwack), 24

Before Color Prejudice: The Ancient View of Blacks (Snowden), 6

Before Freedom Came: African-American Life in the Antebellum South (Campbell),16

Before the Mayflower: A History of Black America (Bennett), 8

Bells of Christmas, The (Hamilton), 105

Bill Cosby: America's Most Famous Father (Haskins), 95

Biographical Dictionary of Afro-American and African Musicians (Southern), 44

Birthday (Steptoe), 107

Black Africans and Native Americans (Forbes), 9

Black American in Books for Children, The: Readings in Racism (MacCann and Woodard), 59

Black American Politics: From the Washington Marches to Jesse Jackson (Marable), 48

Black Americans, The: A History in Their Own Words, 1619–1983 (Meltzer), 87

Black Apollo of Science: The Life of Ernest Everett Just (Manning), 38

Black Art: Ancestral Legacy: The African Impulse in African-American Art (Wardlaw et al.), 44

Black Athena (Bernal), 2

Black Authors and Illustrators of Children's Books: A Biographical Dictionary (Rollock), 61

Black Bostonians: Family Life and Community Struggle in the Antebellum North (Horton and Horton), 21

Black Children: Their Roots, Culture, and Learning Styles (Hale-Benson), 54

Black Church in the African-American Experience, The (Lincoln and Mamiya), 12

Black Cowboys (Stewart and Ponce), 14

Black Dance in America (Haskins), 102

Black Detroit and the Rise of the UAW (Meier and Rudwick), 29

Black Experience in Children's Books, The (New York Public Library), 60

Index of Titles

Black Families: Interdisciplinary Perspectives (Cheatham and Stewart), 46

Black Families in White America (Billingsley), 8

Black Family in Slavery and Freedom, The, 1750–1925 (Gutman), 17

Black Folk Here and There (Drake), 3

Black Folktales (Lester), 116

Black Heroes of the American Revolution (Davis), 92

Black Heroes of the Wild West (Pelz), 98

Black Image in the White Mind, The: The Debate on Afro-American Character and Destiny, 1817–1914 (Frederickson), 10

Black Indians: A Hidden Heritage (Katz), 11

Black Labor in Richmond, 1865–1890 (Rachleff), 27

Black Leaders of the Nineteenth Century (Litwack and Meier), 37

Black Leaders of the Twentieth Century (Franklin and Meier), 35

Black Lives, White Lives: Three Decades of Race Relations in America (Blauner), 46

Black Magic: A Pictorial History of the African American in the Performing Arts (Hughes and Meltzer), 42

Black Masters: A Free Family of Color in the Old South (Johnson and Roark), 22

Black Musical Theatre: From Coontown to Dreamgirls (Woll), 45

Black Music in America: A History through Its People (Haskins), 102

Black Olympian Medalists (Page), 43

Black People Who Made the Old West (Katz), 96

Black Photographers, 1840–1940: An Illustrated Bio-Bibliography (Willis-Thomas), 45

Black Photographers, 1940–1988: An Illustrated Bio-Bibliography (Willis-Thomas), 45

Black Pioneers of Science and Invention (Haber), 94

Black Politicians and Reconstruction in Georgia: A Splendid Failure (Drago), 23

Black Prophets of Justice: Activist Clergy before the Civil War (Swift), 20

Black Protest in the Sixties (Meier, Bracey, and Rudwick), 32

Black Reconstruction (Du Bois), 23

Black Sailors: Afro-American Merchant Seamen and Whalemen prior to the Civil War (Putney), 22

Blacks in American Films and Television: An Encyclopedia (Bogle), 40

Blacks in Antiquity: Ethiopians in the Greco-Roman Experience (Snowden), 6

Blacks in Appalachia (Turner and Cabell), 14

Blacks in the White Establishment? A Study of Race and Class in America (Zweigenhaft and Domhoff), 49

Blacks in Topeka, Kansas, 1865–1915: A Social History (Cox), 26

Black Snowman, The (Mendez), 78

Black Society (Major), 12

Black Theater in America (Haskins), 102

Black Towns and Profit: Promotion and Development in the Trans-Appalachian West, 1877–1915 (Hamilton), 26

Black Tradition in American Dance, The (Long), 43

Black Troubadour: Langston Hughes (Rollins), 100

Black Utopia: Negro Communal Experiments in America (Pease and Pease), 24

Black, White and Southern: Race Relations and Southern Culture, 1940 to the Present (Goldfield), 47

Black Women in America: Social Science Perspectives (Malson et al.), 12

Black Women Writers, 1950–1980: A Critical Evaluation (Evans), 41

Black Workers Selections: A Documentary History from Colonial Times to the Present (Foner and Lewis), 9

Black Writers and the American Civil War (Long), 24

Black Yankees: The Development of an Afro-American Subculture in Eighteenth-Century New England (Piersen), 22

Bloods: An Oral History of the Vietnam War by Black Veterans (Terry), 33

Booker T. Washington (Harlan), 36

Book of Black Heroes: Great Women in the Struggle (Igus), 96

Book of Negro Folklore, The (Hughes and Bontemps), 115

Bo Rabbit Smart for True: Folktales from the Gullah (Jaquith), 115

Borning Room, The (Fleischman), 85

Boy and the Ghost, The (San Souci), 117

Boy Who Didn't Believe in Spring, The (Clifton), 69

Breadsticks and Blessing Places (Boyd), 67

Breaking the Chains: African-American Slave Resistance (Katz), 86

Bright Eyes, Brown Skin (Hudson and Ford), 75

Bringing the Rain to Kapiti Plain: A Nandi Tale (Aardema), 112

Broken Alliance: The Turbulent Times between Blacks and Jews in America (Kaufman), 48

Bronzeville Boys and Girls (Brooks), 67

Brother Anansi and the Cattle Ranch (De Sauza), 114

Brother to the Wind (Walter), 118

Buffalo Soldiers: The 92nd Infantry Division and Reinforcements in World War II, 1942–1945 (Arnold), 28

Bullwhip Days: The Slaves Remember (Mellon), 19

C

Caribbean Canvas (Lessac), 110

Caribbean, The: The Genesis of a Fragmented Nationalism (Knight), 5

Cat's Purr, The (Bryan), 113

Chain Reaction: The Impact of Race, Rights, and Taxes on American Politics (Edsall and Edsall), 47

Charlie Pippin (Boyd), 67

Cherries and Cherry Pits (Williams), 83

Children of Long Ago: Poems (Little), 86

Children of Promise: African-American Literature and Art for Young People (Sullivan), 104

Children of the Wild West (Freedman), 85

Children's Ethnic Socialization (Phinney and Rotheram), 55

Chita's Christmas Tree (Howard), 105

Chronology of African-American History: Significant Events and People from 1619 to the Present (Hornsby), 10

Circle of Gold (Boyd), 67

City Street (Florian), 70

Civilization or Barbarism: An Authentic Anthropology (Diop), 3

Civil Rights Era, The: Origins and Development of National Policy, 1960–1972 (Graham), 31

Civil Rights Movement in America from 1865 to the Present, The (McKissack and McKissack), 87

Claude McKay: Rebel Sojourner in the Harlem Renaissance (Cooper), 35

Climbing Jacob's Ladder: Heroes of the Bible in African-American Spirituals (Langstaff), 103

Climbing Jacob's Ladder: The Rise of Black Churches in Eastern American Cities, 1740–1877 (Smith), 13

Index of Titles

Closing Door, The: Conservative Policy and Black Opportunity (Orfield and Ashkinaze), 48

Coal, Class, and Color: Blacks in Southern West Virginia, 1915–1932 (Trotter), 30

Colin Powell: Straight to the Top (Blue and Naden), 92

Common Destiny, A: Blacks and American Society (Jaynes and Williams), 47

Comprehensive Multicultural Education: Theory and Practice (Bennett), 53

Confessions of Nat Turner, The, Leader of the Late Insurrection in Southampton, Va., As Fully and Voluntarily Made to Thos. C. Gray (Turner), 20

CORE: A Study in the Civil Rights Movement, 1942–1968 (Meier and Rudwick), 32

Cornrows (Yarbrough), 84

Count on Your Fingers African Style (Zaslavsky), 112

Country Far Away, A (Gray), 108

Cousins (Hamilton), 74

Crusade for Justice: The Autobiography of Ida B. Wells (Wells), 40

Cultural Conformity in Books for Children: Further Readings in Racism (MacCann and Woodard), 60

Culture, Style, and the Educative Process (Shade), 56

Curriculum Guidelines for Multicultural Education: Position Statement (National Council for the Social Studies), 55

D

Dancing Granny, The (Bryan), 113

Daniel's Dog (Bogart), 67

Dark Journey: Black Mississippians in the Age of Jim Crow (McMillen), 29

Darkness and the Butterfly (Grifalconi), 109

Darlene (Greenfield), 71

David Walker's Appeal (Walker), 20

Daydreamers (Greenfield), 71

Day of Ahmed's Secret, The (Heide and Gilliland), 110

Death and Life of Malcolm X, The (Goldman), 36

Destruction of Black Civilization, The: Great Issues of a Race from 4500 B.C. to 2000 A.D. (Williams), 7

Developing the Multicultural Process in Classroom Instruction: Competencies for Teachers (Baptiste and Baptiste), 57

Development of Black Theater in America, The: From Shadows to Selves (Sanders), 44

Diary of a Sit-in (Proudfoot), 33

Dictionary of American Negro Biography (Logan and Winston), 12

Different and Wonderful: Raising Black Children in a Race-Conscious Society (Powell-Hopson and Hopson), 49

Different Kind of Christmas, A (Haley), 105

Diversity in the Classroom: A Multicultural Approach to the Education of Young Children (Kendall), 59

Documentary History of the Negro People in the United States, A (Aptheker), 7

Do Like Kyla (Johnson), 76

Don't Explain: A Song of Billie Holiday (De Veaux), 93

Don't You Remember? (Clifton), 105

Double Dutch (Walker and Haskins), 104

Down by the Riverside: A South Carolina Slave Community (Joyner), 18

Dr. Martin Luther King, Jr.: Man of Peace (Patterson), 98

Dream Keeper and Other Poems (Hughes), 76

Dream Long Deferred, The (Gaillard), 47

Duey's Tale (Bailey), 66

Dust Tracks on the Road: An Autobiography (Hurston), 37

E

Education of Black People, The: Ten Critiques, 1906–1960 (Du Bois), 9

Education of Blacks in the South, The, 1860–1935 (Anderson), 7

Education of the Negro in the American Social Order, The (Bond), 8

Efan the Great (Schotter), 107

Ego-tripping and Other Poems for Young People (Giovanni), 71

Egypt Revisited (Van Sertima), 6

Ellington: The Early Years (Tucker), 39

Emperor Shaka the Great (Kunene), 5

Empowerment through Multicultural Education (Sleeter), 56

Enchanted Hair Tale, An (De Veaux), 70

Encyclopedia of Black America (Low and Clift), 12

Encyclopedia of Southern Culture (Wilson and Ferris), 14

Engaging the Battle for African-American Minds (Shade), 55

Escape to Freedom: A Play about Young Frederick Douglass (Davis), 93

Everett Anderson's Friend (Clifton), 69

Everett Anderson's Goodbye (Clifton), 69

Everett Anderson's Nine Month Long (Clifton), 69

Extraordinary Black Americans from Colonial to Contemporary Times (Altman), 91

Eyes on the Prize: America's Civil Rights Years, 1954–1965 (Williams), 34

F

Facing History: The Black Image in American Art, 1710–1940 (McElroy and Gates), 43

Fallen Angels (Myers), 88

Family Life and School Achievement: Why Poor Black Children Succeed or Fail (Clark), 53

Famous Firsts of Black Americans (Hancock), 94

Fast Sam, Cool Clyde, and Stuff (Myers), 79

Finding the Green Stone (Walker), 82

Fire Next Time, The (Baldwin), 45

First Pink Light (Greenfield), 72

Follow the Drinking Gourd (Winter), 90

Forged in Battle: The Civil War Alliance of Black Soldiers and White Officers (Glatthaar), 24

Frederick Douglass (McFeely), 38

Frederick Douglass' Civil War: Keeping Faith in Jubilee (Blight), 35

Frederick Douglass: The Black Lion (McKissack and McKissack), 97

Free Black in Urban America, The, 1800–1850: The Shadow of the Dream (Curry), 21

Freedom: A Documentary History of Emancipation, 1861–1867 (Berlin et al.), 22

Freedom Bound: A History of America's Civil Rights Movement (Weisbrot), 34

Freedom Songs (Moore), 88

Freedom Summer (McAdam), 32

Free Frank: A Black Pioneer on the Antebellum Frontier (Walker), 39

Friendship, The (Taylor), 89

Friends, The (Guy), 73

Fritz Pollard: Pioneer in Racial Advancement (Carroll), 35

From Harlem to Paris: Black American Writers in France, 1840–1980 (Fabre), 42

From Slavery to Freedom: A History of Negro Americans (Franklin and Moss), 9

From Trickster to Badman: The Black Folk Hero in Slavery and Freedom (Roberts), 44

Index of Titles

Further Tales of Uncle Remus: The Misadventures of Brer Rabbit, Brer Fox, Brer Wolf, the Doodang, and All the Other Creatures (Lester and Fogelman), 117

G

Gift-Giver, The (Hansen), 74

Go Fish (Stolz), 81

Gold Cadillac, The (Taylor), 90

Golden Pasture, The (Thomas), 82

Grandma's Baseball (Curtis), 69

Grandpa's Face (Greenfield), 72

Great Black Leaders, Ancient and Modern (Van Sertima), 39

Green Lion of Zion Street, The (Fields), 70

Growing Up Literate: Learning from Inner-City Families (Taylor and Dorsey-Gaines), 56

H

Half a Moon and One Whole Star (Dragonwagon), 70

Hard Road to Glory, A: The History of the African-American Athlete (Ashe), 40

Harlem Renaissance, The: An Historical Dictionary for the Era (Kellner), 43

Harold Washington: Mayor with a Vision (Roberts), 99

Harriet Tubman (Bentley), 91

Harriet Tubman: Conductor on the Underground Railroad (Petry), 98

Harvard Encyclopedia of American Ethnic Groups (Thernstrom, Orlov, and Handlin), 56

Have a Happy . . . (Walter), 107

Hearth and Home: Preserving a People's Culture (McDaniel), 26

Hero Ain't Nothing But a Sandwich, A (Childress), 68

Historical and Cultural Atlas of African Americans (Asante and Mattson), 7

Historic Landmarks of Black America (Cantor), 9

History of West Africa (Ajayi and Crowder), 2

Home Place (Dragonwagon), 70

Honey, I Love, and Other Love Poems (Greenfield), 71

House of Dies Drear, The (Hamilton), 85

Housing Status of Black Americans, The (Leigh and Stewart), 48

How Europe Underdeveloped Africa (Rodney), 5

How Many Spots Does a Leopard Have? And Other Tales (Lester), 116

How the Leopard Got His Claws (Achebe and Iroaganachi), 113

Hundred Penny Box, The (Mathis), 77

I

I Am a Jesse White Tumbler (Schmidt), 104

Iggie's House (Blume), 66

I Know Why the Caged Bird Sings (Angelou), 34

Image of the Black in Children's Fiction, The (Broderick), 57

Image of the Black in Western Art, The (Vercoutter et al.), 44

I'm Going to Sing: Black American Spirituals (Bryan), 101

I Need a Lunch Box (Caines), 68

I Never Had It Made: The Autobiography of Jackie Robinson (Robinson), 99

Infusion Model for Teaching Dr. Martin Luther King, Jr.'s Nonviolent Principles in Schools (Martin Luther King, Jr., Center for Nonviolent Social Change), 60

In Struggle: SNCC and the Black Awakening of the 1960s (Carson), 30

Introduction to African Civilizations (Jackson), 5

Invisible Empire in the West, The: Toward a New Historical Appraisal of the Ku Klux Klan of the 1920s (Lay), 29

J

Jafta (Lewin), 110

Jamal's Busy Day (Hudson), 75

Jambo Means Hello: Swahili Alphabet Book (Feelings), 108

Jazz Cleopatra: Josephine Baker in Her Time (Rose), 39

Jenny (Wilson), 84

Jesse Jackson: A Biography (McKissack), 97

Jesse Jackson's 1984 Presidential Campaign: Challenge and Change in American Politics (Barker and Walters), 46

Jim Beckwourth: Black Trapper and Indian Chief (Blassingame), 92

Journal of a Residence on a Georgian Plantation in 1838–1839 (Kemble), 18

Journey to Jo'Burg: A South African Story (Naidoo), 111

Jump on Over! The Adventures of Brer Rabbit and His Family (Harris), 115

Justin and the Best Biscuits in the World (Walter), 82

Just Us Women (Caines), 68

K

Keeping the Faith: A. Philip Randolph, Milton P. Webster, and the Brotherhood of Sleeping Car Porters, 1925–1937 (Harris), 29

Kwanzaa (Chocolate), 105

Kwanzaa (Porter), 107

Kwanzaa: Everything You Always Wanted to Know But Didn't Know Where to Ask (McClester), 106

L

Labor of Love, Labor of Sorrow: Black Women, Work, and the Family from Slavery to the Present (Jones), 11

Langston: A Play (Davis), 93

Last Summer with Maizon (Woodson), 84

Legend of Africania, The (Robinson), 117

Lena Horne (Haskins), 95

Let It Burn! The Philadelphia Tragedy (Boyette and Boyette), 46

Let the Circle Be Unbroken (Taylor), 89

Let the Trumpet Sound: The Life of Martin Luther King, Jr. (Oates), 38

Life of Langston Hughes, The (Rampersad), 38

Lillian Smith: A Southerner Confronting the South (Loveland), 37

Lincoln and Black Freedom: A Study in Presidential Leadership (Cox), 23

Lion and the Ostrich Chicks, and Other African Folktales (Bryan), 113

Listen Children: An Anthology of Black Literature (Strickland), 104

Lives of Jean Toomer, The: A Hunger for Wholeness (Kerman and Eldridge), 37

Long Hard Journey, A: The Story of the Pullman Porter (McKissack and McKissack), 87

Long Memory: The Black Experience in America (Berry and Blassingame), 8

Lord of the Dance: An African Retelling (Tadjo), 111

Louis Armstrong (Tanenhaus), 101

Louis Armstrong: An American Success Story (Collier), 92

Ludell (Wilkinson), 83

Ludell and Willie (Wilkinson), 83

Ludell's New York Time (Wilkinson), 83

M

M.C. Higgins, the Great (Hamilton), 73

Maggie's American Dream: The Life and Times of a Black Family (Comer), 28

Major Butler's Legacy: Five Generations of a Slaveholding Family (Bell), 15

Making Choices for Multicultural Education: Five Approaches to Race, Class, and Gender (Sleeter and Grant), 56

Making of Black Revolutionaries, The: A Personal Account (Forman), 31

Malcolm X and Black Pride (Cwiklik), 92

Marching to Freedom: The Story of Martin Luther King, Jr. (Milton), 98

Mariah Loves Rock (Walter), 83

Marian Anderson (Patterson), 98

Marked by Fire (Thomas), 81

Martin Luther King Day (Lowery), 106

Martin Luther King, Jr. (Smith), 100

Mary Had a Little Lamb (Hale), 114

Mary McLeod Bethune: A Great American Educator (McKissack), 97

Matthew Henson (Gilman), 94

Me, Mop and the Moondance Kid (Myers), 79

Mirandy and Brother Wind (McKissack), 78

Miseducation of the Negro, The (Woodson), 14

Mississippi Bridge (Taylor), 90

Mob Intent on Death, A: The NAACP and the Arkansas Riot Cases (Cortner), 28

Modern Caribbean, The (Knight and Palmer), 5

Moja Means One: Swahili Counting Book (Feelings), 108

More Tales of Uncle Remus: Further Adventures of Brer Rabbit, His Friends, Enemies and Others (Lester), 116

Mother Crocodile: An Uncle Amadou Tale from Senegal (Guy), 114

Motown and Didi: A Love Story (Myers), 79

Mufaro's Beautiful Daughters: An African Tale (Steptoe), 118

Multicolored Mirror, The: Cultural Substance in Literature for Children and Young Adults (Cooperative Children's Book Center), 58

Multicultural Classroom, The: Readings for Content-Area Teachers (Richard-Amato and Snow), 55

Multicultural Education: A Source Book (Ramsey), 60

Multicultural Education: A Synopsis (Baptiste), 53

Multicultural Education: A Teacher's Guide to Content and Process (Hernandez), 54

Multicultural Education in a Pluralistic Society (Gollnick and Chinn), 54

Multicultural Education in Western Societies (Banks and Lynch), 52

Multicultural Education: Issues and Perspectives (Banks and Banks), 52

Multicultural Education of Children and Adolescents (Baruth and Manning), 53

Multicultural Education: Product and Process (Boyer), 53

Multicultural Literature for Children and Young Adults (Cooperative Children's Book Center), 58

Multicultural Teaching: A Handbook of Activities, Information, and Resources (Tiedt and Tiedt), 61

Multiethnic Education: Theory and Practice (Banks), 52

Mutiny on the Amistad: The Saga of a Slave Revolt and Its Impact on American Abolition, Law, and Diplomacy (James), 17

My Black Me: A Beginning Book of Black Poetry (Adoff), 66

My Friend Jacob (Clifton), 69

My Mama Needs Me (Walter), 82

My Name Is Not Angelica (O'Dell), 88

Mystery of Drear House, The: The Conclusion of the Dies Drear Chronicle (Hamilton), 86

N

NAACP Crusade against Lynching, The, 1909–1950 (Zangrando), 34

NAACP's Legal Strategy against Segregated Education, The, 1925–1950 (Tushnet), 34

Narrative of the Life of Frederick Douglass, An American Slave (Douglass), 35

Nathaniel Talking (Greenfield), 72

Necessary Evil, A? Slavery and the Debate over the Constitution (Kaminski and Leffler), 18

Necessities: Racial Barriers in American Sports (Hoose), 42

Negro Almanac, The: A Reference Work on the African American (Ploski and Williams), 13

Negro Caravan, The (Brown, Davis, and Lee), 41

Negro in Our History, The (Woodson and Wesley), 14

Negro in the Making of America, The (Quarles), 13

Nelson Mandela (Feinberg), 93

New Cavalcade, The: African-American Writing from 1760 to the Present (Davis, Redding, and Joyce), 41

New Directions in Civil Rights Studies (Robinson and Sullivan), 33

Not So Fast, Songololo (Daly), 108

Now Is Your Time! The African-American Struggle for Freedom (Myers), 88

Ntombi's Song (Seed), 111

O

Once Upon a Time When We Were Colored (Taulbert), 30

One of Three (Johnson), 76

Only the Ball Was White: A History of Legendary Black Players and All-Black Professional Teams (Peterson), 43

Open Minds to Equality: A Sourcebook of Learning Activities to Promote Race, Sex, Class, and Age Equity (Schniedewind and Davidson), 61

Origins of the Civil Rights Movement, The: Black Communities Organizing for Change (Morris), 33

Orphan Boy, The (Mollel), 117

Osa's Pride (Grifalconi), 109

Our Martin Luther King Book (McKissack), 106

OUTside INside Poems (Adoff), 66

P

P.B. Young, Newspaperman: Race, Politics, and Journalism in the New South, 1910–1962 (Suggs), 39

Painting Faces (Haldane), 102

Paper Bird: A Novel of South Africa (Maartens), 110

Papers of Martin Luther King, Jr., The: Called to Serve, January 1929–June 1951 (Carson, Luker, and Russell), 31

Paris, Pee Wee, and Big Dog (Guy), 73

Parting the Waters: America in the King Years, 1954–1963 (Branch), 30

Patchwork Quilt, The (Flournoy), 71

Pauli Murray: The Autobiography of a Black Activist, Feminist, Lawyer, Priest, and Poet (Murray), 38

Paul Robeson (Duberman), 35

Paul Robeson: Hero before His Time (Larsen), 96

Peculiar People, A: Slave Religion and Community Culture among the Gullah (Creel), 16

People Could Fly, The: American Black Folktales (Hamilton), 115

Picture Book of Martin Luther King, Jr., A (Adler), 91

Planning and Organizing for Multicultural Instruction (Baker), 52

Plays from African Folktales: With Ideas for Acting, Dance, Costumes, and Music (Korty), 116

Port Chicago Mutiny, The (Allen), 27

Pride of Family: Four Generations of American Women of Color (Ione), 11

Proceedings of Black State Conventions, 1840–1865 (Foner and Walker), 21

Promised Land, The: The Great Black Migration and How It Changed America (Lemann), 29

Promiseland: A Century of Life in a Negro Community (Bethel), 22

Pursuit of a Dream, The (Hermann), 24

Q

Question of Sedition, A: The Federal Government's Investigation of the Black Press during World War II (Washburn), 30

Quilt, The (Jonas), 77

R

Rabbit Makes a Monkey of Lion: A Swahili Tale (Aardema), 112

Race and Kinship in a Midwestern Town: The Black Experience in Monroe, Michigan, 1900–1915 (De Vries), 26

Race and Revolution (Nash), 19

Race, Religion, and the Continuing American Dilemma (Lincoln), 12

Ragtime Tumpie (Schroeder), 100

Rainbow Jordan (Childress), 68

Rain Talk (Serfozo), 80

Ray Charles (Mathis), 97

Real McCoy, The: African-American Invention and Innovation, 1619–1930 (James), 11

Reconstruction: America's Unfinished Revolution, 1863–1877 (Foner), 23

Red, White, and Black: The Peoples of Early America (Nash), 19

Reflections of an Affirmative Action Baby (Carter), 46

Rehema's Journey: A Visit in Tanzania (Margolies), 111

Reshaping of Plantation Society, The: The Natchez District, 1860–1880 (Wayne), 25

Resources for Educational Equity: An Annotated Bibliography and Guide for Grades Pre-Kindergarten–12 (Froschl and Sprung), 58

Rice and Slaves: Ethnicity and the Slave Trade in Colonial South Carolina (Littlefield), 18

Richard Allen: Religious Leader and Social Activist (Klots), 96

Road to Bethlehem, The: An Ethiopian Nativity (Laird), 106

Road to Memphis, The (Taylor), 90

Rock in a Weary Land, A: The African Methodist Episcopal Church during the Civil War and Reconstruction (Walker), 25

Roll of Thunder, Hear My Cry (Taylor), 89

Rosa Parks and the Montgomery Bus Boycott (Celsi), 92

S

Sable Arm, The: Black Troops in the Union Army, 1861–1865 (Cornish), 23

Samuel's Choice (Berleth), 84

Satchel Paige (Humphrey), 96

Savage Inequalities: Children in America's Schools (Kozol), 48

Scott Joplin (Preston), 99

Scramble for Africa, The, 1876–1912 (Pakenham), 5

Secret of Gumbo Grove, The (Tate), 81

Seventeen Black Artists (Fax), 93

Shades of Black: Diversity in African-American Identity (Cross), 47

Shadow of Slavery, The: Peonage in the South, 1901–1969 (Daniel), 28

Shaka: King of the Zulus (Stanley and Vennema), 100

Shake It to the One That You Love the Best: Play Songs and Lullabies from Black Musical Traditions (Mattox), 103

Shaping of Black America, The (Bennett), 8

Sharing Traditions: Five Black Artists in Nineteenth-Century America (Hartigan), 42

Shimmershine Queens, The (Yarbrough), 84

Shirley Chisholm: Teacher and Congresswoman (Scheader), 100

Sidewalk Story (Mathis), 77

Simple Justice: The History of Brown v. Board of Education and Black America's Struggle for Equality (Kluger), 32

Sister (Greenfield), 72

Slave Community, The: Plantation Life in the Antebellum South (Blassingame), 15

Slave Culture: Nationalist Theory and the Foundations of Black America (Stuckey), 20

Slavery and Freedom in the Age of the American Revolution (Berlin and Hoffman), 15

Slavery and Human Progress (Davis), 16

Slave Ship, The (Sterne), 89

Sojourner Truth and the Voice of Freedom (Shumate), 100

Something on My Mind (Grimes), 73

Something to Count On (Moore), 79

Song in Stone, A: City Poems (Hopkins), 74

Song of the Trees (Taylor), 89

Sorrow's Kitchen: The Life and Folklore of Zora Neale Hurston (Lyons), 96

Soul Brothers and Sister Lou, The (Hunter), 76

Souls of Black Folk, The (Du Bois), 26

Southern Black Leaders of the Reconstruction Era (Rabinowitz), 25

Space Challenger: The Story of Guion Bluford (Haskins and Benson), 95

Spin a Soft Black Song: Poems for Children (Giovanni), 71

Split Image: African Americans in the Mass Media (Dates and Barlow), 41

. . . Starting School (Ahlberg), 66

State of Afro-American History, The: Past, Present and Future (Hine), 10

Stevie (Steptoe), 80

Stony Road: Chapters in the History of Hampton Institute (Schall), 29

Storm in the Night (Stolz), 81

Story, a Story, A: An African Tale (Haley), 114

Story of Stevie Wonder, The (Haskins), 95

Straight from the Heart (Jackson), 47

Strange Career of Jim Crow, The (Woodward), 27

Strength for the Fight: A History of Black Americans in the Military (Nalty), 12

Sweet Whispers, Brother Rush (Hamilton), 73

T

Take a Walk in Their Shoes (Turner), 101

Taking a Stand against Racism and Racial Discrimination (McKissack and McKissack), 78

Tales of Uncle Remus, The: The Adventures of Brer Rabbit (Lester), 116

Talking Eggs, The (San Souci), 118

Talk That Talk: An Anthology of African-American Storytelling (Goss and Barnes), 42

Tar Beach (Ringgold), 80

Teaching and Learning in a Diverse World: Multicultural Education for Young Children (Ramsey), 60

Teaching Ethnic and Gender Awareness: Methods and Materials for the Elementary School (King), 59

Teaching in a Pluralistic Society: Concepts, Models, Strategies (Garcia), 54

Index of Titles

Teaching Minorities More Effectively: A Model for Educators (Brown), 57

Teaching Strategies for Ethnic Studies (Banks), 52

Teacup Full of Roses (Mathis), 78

Teammates (Golenbock), 102

Tears for Ashan (Marie), 87

Telling Tales: The Pedagogy and Promise of African American Literature for Youth (Johnson), 59

Tell Me a Story, Mama (Johnson), 76

Thank You, Dr. Martin Luther King, Jr.! (Tate), 81

There Is a River: The Black Struggle for Freedom in America (Harding), 17

They Came before Columbus: The African Presence in Ancient America (Van Sertima), 14

They're All Named Wildfire (Springer), 80

They Who Would Be Free: Blacks' Search for Freedom, 1830–1861 (Pease and Pease), 19

Thief in the Village and Other Stories of Jamaica, A (Berry), 107

This Life (Poitier), 99

This Species of Property: Slave Life and Culture in the Old South (Owens), 19

This Strange New Feeling (Lester), 86

Thomas Morris Chester, Black Civil War Correspondent: His Dispatches from the Virginia Front (Blackett), 34

Thurgood Marshall (Aldred), 91

Tituba of Salem Village (Petry), 98

Tobacco and Slaves: The Development of Southern Culture in the Chesapeake, 1680–1800 (Kulikoff), 18

To Be a Slave (Lester), 86

Tommy Traveller in the World of Black History (Feelings), 85

To Tell a Free Story: The First Century of Afro-American Autobiography, 1760–1865 (Andrews), 40

Town That Started the Civil War, The (Brandt), 16

Train to Lulu's, The (Howard), 75

Traveling to Tondo: A Tale of the Nkundo of Zaire (Aardema), 113

Trek, The (Jonas), 77

Trouble's Child (Walter), 82

Truly Disadvantaged, The: The Inner City, the Underclass, and Public Policy (Wilson), 49

Trumpet of Conscience, The (King), 32

Turning on Learning (Grant and Sleeter), 58

Turtle Knows Your Name (Bryan), 114

Twentieth-Century African-American Writers and Artists (Hedgepeth), 42

U

Uncommon Ground: Archaeology and Colonial African America (Ferguson), 17

Underground Man (Meltzer), 88

Underground Railroad, The: First-Person Narratives of Escapes to Freedom in the North (Blockson), 16

Under the Sunday Tree (Greenfield), 109

UNESCO General History of Africa, The (International Scientific Committee for the Drafting of a General History of Africa), 4

Up from Slavery (Washington), 40

Ups and Downs of Carl Davis III, The (Guy), 73

Urban Underclass, The (Jencks and Peterson), 48

V

Village of Round and Square Houses, The (Grifalconi), 109

Violence in the Model City: The Cavanaugh Administration, Race Relations, and the Detroit Riot of 1967 (Fine), 28

Visit to the Country, A (Johnson), 77

Voice of Deliverance: The Language of Martin Luther King, Jr., and Its Sources (Miller), 33

Voices of Freedom: An Oral History of the Civil Rights Movement from the 1950s through the 1980s (Hampton and Fayer), 31

W

W.E.B. Du Bois: A Biography (Hamilton), 94

Waiting for the Rain: A Novel of South Africa (Gordon), 108

Walking the Road to Freedom: A Story about Sojourner Truth (Ferris), 93

Wave in Her Pocket, A: Stories from Trinidad (Joseph), 110

We Are Your Sisters: Black Women in the Nineteenth Century (Sterling), 13

We Keep a Store (Shelby), 80

What a Morning! The Christmas Story in Black Spirituals (Langstaff), 106

When and Where I Enter: The Impact of Black Women on Race and Sex in America (Giddings), 10

When I Am Old with You (Johnson), 76

When Roots Die: Endangered Traditions on the Sea Islands (Jones-Jackson), 11

White over Black: American Attitudes toward the Negro, 1550–1812 (Jordan), 18

White Violence and Black Response: From Reconstruction to Montgomery (Shapiro), 13

Whose Side Are You On? (Moore), 78

Who's in Rabbit's House: A Masai Tale (Aardema), 112

Why Mosquitoes Buzz in People's Ears: A West African Tale (Aardema), 112

Why We Can't Wait (King), 32

Wild Wild Sunflower Child Anna (Carlstrom), 68

Willie Bea and the Time the Martians Landed (Hamilton), 85

Within the Plantation Household: Black and White Women of the Old South (Fox-Genovese), 17

Wonderful World of Difference, The (Anti-Defamation League of B'nai B'rith), 57

Working with Carter G. Woodson, the Father of Black History: A Diary, 1928–1930 (Greene), 36

World and Africa, The: An Inquiry into the Part Which Africa Has Played in World History (Du Bois), 4

World They Made Together, The: Black and White Values in Eighteenth-Century Virginia (Sobel), 20

Y

Yellow Bird and Me (Hansen), 74

You May Plow Here: The Narrative of Sara Brooks (Simonsen), 39

Young Landlords, The (Myers), 79